Minimalist Baker's Everyday Cooking

Minimalist Baker's Everyday Cooking

101 entirely plant-based, mostly gluten-free, easy and delicious recipes

DANA SHULTZ

author of Minimalist Baker

AVERY

an imprint of Penguin Random House

New York

An imprint of Penguin Random House LLC
375 Hudson Street
New York, New York 10014

Most Avery books are available at special quantity discounts for
bulk purchase for sales promotions, premiums, fund-raising, and educational
needs. Special books or book excerpts also can be created to fit specific
needs. For details, write SpecialMarkets@penguinrandomhouse.com.

ISBN 9780735210967

Printed in the United States of America
1 3 5 7 9 10 8 6 4 2

Book design by Holly Whittlef, hollisanne.com

Author photographs taken by Allison Wonderland, wonderlass.com

This book is dedicated to anyone who has ever made
a recipe from Minimalist Baker, shared our blog with a
friend, brought one of our dishes to a gathering, sung
our praises, or simply sent us a kind e-mail to say hello.
You are our fans, and we're oh so grateful for you.

We hope you love this cookbook as much as we do.

Contents

Introduction

DANA | JOHN

SHE BRAINS | **HE BRAINS**

1 BOWL

30 MINUTES OR LESS

10 INGREDIENTS OR LESS

GLUTEN-FREE

MINIMALISTBAKER.COM

MINIMALIST BAKER IS A BLOG and online community devoted to simple cooking.

Born out of a passion for easy-to-make, delicious food, all recipes either require 10 ingredients or less, 1 bowl or 1 pot, or 30 minutes or less to prepare.

HOW DID IT START?

I have loved food with all of my being since childhood, so it was only a matter of time before I discovered a way to make a career out of eating.

I began reading food blogs in college but always struggled to find recipes that didn't require an excess of time, money, and energy to prepare. So I decided to make the blog I wanted to read and cook from.

With my appetite for simple food and my husband John's business sense and knack for website design, we combined our skills to create Minimalist Baker in June 2012. An idea that started over a simple conversation at dinner has since morphed into a full-blown creative passion and thriving business.

On a daily basis, I handle the cooking, writing, and photography, while John manages the branding, growth strategy, and technical side of the blog. Together, we make a pretty good pair and have a lot of fun.

WHY PLANT-BASED?
Despite being raised in Midwestern, meat-eating homes, both John and I found ourselves dabbling in veganism and vegetarianism throughout college, primarily for health reasons.

Throw in my lactose intolerance, and you'll find that we—despite not subscribing to any one diet—enjoy eating and cooking mostly plant-based meals.

I FIND IT VERY REWARDING TO CREATE RECIPES THAT TASTE JUST AS GOOD AS THE ORIGINAL, WHILE STILL REMAINING PLANT-BASED.

Because of my sensitivity to dairy, I have been experimenting with dairy-free and egg-free baking for many years. I find it very rewarding to create recipes that taste just as good as the original, while still remaining plant-based. Throughout this process, vegan and gluten-free cooking have become my passion.

WHAT TO EXPECT

For quite some time our readers have requested a print cookbook they could hold in their hands and cook from every day, something that didn't require a screen, and could sit in the kitchen, ready to be used.

This cookbook is our response to that request, and we are so excited to present to you this collection of 101 entirely plant-based, mostly gluten-free, easy and delicious recipes.

The "everyday" in the title implies practicality, as the recipes in this book are designed for everyday use.

Think entrées, side dishes, appetizers, and breakfast recipes, with a few desserts and drinks sprinkled in for good measure.

We hope you enjoy this book as much as we enjoyed creating it, and we truly hope you put it to good use. It would make us happy to have this cookbook become your trusty kitchen companion. Please wrinkle the pages, dust it with crumbs, and use it often.

With love,
DANA & JOHN

Resources

BOOKMARK THIS SECTION! IT'S A small but essential collection of how-tos and vegan cooking resources.

In this section you'll find step-by-step instructions on how to make ingredients that are frequently used in the recipes in this cookbook. Ingredients include flax eggs (a vegan substitute for chicken eggs in baking) (see Flax Egg, page 6), DIY Almond Milk (page 6), Coconut Whipped Cream (page 8), and Vegan Parmesan (page 7).

You'll also find a few other staple recipes and cooking shortcuts that will come in handy as you work your way through the cookbook.

Good luck!

FLAX EGG *page 6*

Throughout the cookbook you'll notice labels in the top corner of each recipe indicating its "simple factor" and whether or not it is gluten-free. I hope you find these useful as you plan out your meals and enjoy each dish.

> *1 BOWL OR POT
>
> *30 MINUTES OR LESS
>
> *10 INGREDIENTS OR LESS
>
> *GF GLUTEN-FREE

NOTE: Know that "10 ingredients or less" does not include water or optional ingredients.

VEGAN PARMESAN *page 7*

COCONUT WHIPPED CREAM *page 8*

Flax Egg

MAKES 1 FLAX EGG

1 Tbsp (7g) flaxseed meal (ground raw flaxseed)

2½ Tbsp (37ml) water

01 Combine the flaxseed meal and water in a small bowl and stir. Let rest for 5 minutes to thicken. Add to recipes in place of 1 small chicken egg.

02 This is not an exact 1:1 substitution in every recipe because it does not bind and stiffen during baking quite like an egg does. But I've found it works incredibly well in pancakes, quick breads, brownies, muffins, cookies, and many other recipes.

DIY Almond Milk

MAKES 5 CUPS

1 cup (112g) raw almonds (soaked in cool water for 4 to 6 hours, or 1 hour in very hot water, then drained)

5 cups (1,200ml) filtered water (less for thicker milk, more for thinner milk)

2 dates, pitted, or other sweetener of choice (omit for unsweetened)

1 tsp pure vanilla extract or 1 vanilla bean, scraped (omit for plain)

Pinch of sea salt

01 Add the soaked almonds, water, dates, vanilla, and salt to the bowl of a high-speed blender. Blend until creamy and smooth. Keep blending for at least 1-2 minutes to get the most out of the almonds.

02 Strain using a nut milk bag or thin dish towel. Simply lay a clean dish towel over a bowl, pour the almond milk over the dish towel, carefully gather the corners, and lift up. Then squeeze until all of the liquid is extracted. Compost the pulp or save for adding to baked goods.

03 Transfer the almond milk to a jar or covered bottle. Refrigerate. The almond milk will keep for 3-4 days. Shake well before using as it tends to separate.

04 Flavors can also be infused. For strawberry, add 5-6 hulled strawberries when blending. For chocolate, add 1-2 Tbsp (5-10g) cacao or unsweetened cocoa powder.

Gluten-Free Flour Blend

MAKES 2½ CUPS (400g)

PREP TIME 5 MIN. | TOTAL TIME 5 MIN.

1½ cups (240g)
brown rice flour

½ cup (96g) potato starch

¼ cup (40g) white
rice flour

¼ cup (30g) tapioca flour

OPTIONAL
1 tsp xanthan gum*
(for binding)

01 Whisk the brown rice flour, potato starch, white rice flour, and tapioca flour together in a large bowl. Store in an airtight container in a dry place (I use a large mason jar). Lasts for several months.

02 Gluten-free flours can be tricky because they react differently in pretty much every recipe. With that in mind, use this blend in place of all-purpose or whole wheat flour.

Notes

*For extra binding (since gluten is not present), add a pinch of xanthan gum, depending on the recipe, though I don't find it absolutely necessary.

TIP: I have found substituting gluten-free flour in place of all-purpose flour in a 1:1 ratio doesn't always yield the best results. Because of this, I recommend including other ingredients, such as almond meal, oat flour, and/or rolled oats, in addition to the gluten-free blend, to create a more desirable texture.

EXAMPLE: If a recipe calls for 1 cup (136g) all-purpose flour, I generally substitute ½ cup gluten-free flour blend (80g), ¼ cup gluten-free oat flour (23g), and ¼ cup almond meal (27g), depending on the recipe.

This blend has worked wonders for me in muffins, cakes, quick breads, cornbread, waffles, gluten-free crêpes, and more.

Vegan Parmesan

MAKES 1 CUP

PREP TIME 5 MIN. | TOTAL TIME 5 MIN.

¾ cup (90g) raw cashews

3 Tbsp (9g)
nutritional yeast

¼ tsp sea salt

¼ tsp garlic powder

01 Add all of the ingredients to the bowl of a food processor. Mix/pulse until a fine meal is achieved. Store in the refrigerator to keep fresh. Lasts for several weeks.

02 I love vegan parmesan on top of pizza, pastas, avocado toast, gratins, and more. It also adds flavor and helps thickens creamy pasta sauces.

Coconut Whipped Cream

MAKES 2 CUPS

1 14-ounce (414ml) can coconut cream or full-fat coconut milk*

½ tsp pure vanilla extract

4-6 Tbsp (28-42g) organic powdered sugar

Notes

*I've found not all coconut creams and milks are created equal. Some have varied fat content and remain too liquid even after chilling, which prevents whipping. The best brands I've found are *Trader Joe's coconut cream*, *Thai Kitchen full-fat coconut milk*, and *Whole Foods 365 full-fat coconut milk*.

*If your coconut milk doesn't harden after chilling, it's possibly a dud can without the right fat content (see above note). You can try to salvage it with tapioca flour–1-4 Tbsp (7½-30g)– during the whipping process. I've found, however, this doesn't always work.

PREP TIME 10 MIN.* | TOTAL TIME 10 MIN.

01 Chill the coconut cream in the refrigerator overnight.

02 Remove the can from the refrigerator without tipping or shaking it. Remove the lid. Scrape out the top portion of cream that has thickened, leaving the liquid behind.

03 Place the cream in a large bowl that has been chilled for 10 minutes. Beat for 30 seconds using a handheld mixer until creamy. Add the vanilla and powdered sugar 1 Tbsp (7g) at a time. Beat until creamy and smooth, about 1 minute.

04 Use immediately or refrigerate. It will firm up and stiffen the longer it's chilled. Will keep for 1-2 weeks.

05 Coconut whipped cream is perfect for topping pie, hot cocoa, ice cream, and more.

Prep time does not include chilling the coconut cream.

Cauliflower Rice

MAKES 3-4 CUPS

1 head of cauliflower, stems removed, quartered

1 Tbsp (15ml) grape seed oil or toasted sesame oil

TIP: Serve as is or season with 1-2 Tbsp desired sauce for more flavor. This recipe is a great substitute for traditional rice in Mexican, Indian, Asian, and other dishes.

PREP TIME 5 MIN. | TOTAL TIME 12 MIN.

01 Heat a large skillet over medium to medium-high heat.

02 Shred the cauliflower into "rice" using a large box grater or food processor with a fine blade. It should resemble the size of rice.

03 Once the skillet is hot, add the grape seed oil to the skillet, then add the cauliflower rice. Stir. Cover to steam and cook for 4-7 minutes total, or until slightly browned and tender, stirring occasionally.

Roasted Garlic

MAKES 1 HEAD OF GARLIC

1 head of garlic

1 tsp grape seed oil

Pinch of sea salt

PREP TIME 5 MIN. | TOTAL TIME 1 HR. 5 MIN.

01 Preheat the oven to 400 degrees F (204 degrees C). Cut off the very top of the head of garlic. Drizzle the top with grape seed oil and a sprinkle of salt. Loosely wrap in foil.

02 Place directly on the oven rack and roast for 45 minutes to 1 hour, depending on the size of the garlic. It is done when fragrant and the bulb appears soft and golden brown. Remove from the oven and let cool.

03 Once cooled, squeeze from the base to push the softened cloves out the top. Use immediately, or store in a jar with enough grape seed or olive oil to cover. Garlic will keep for several weeks or more.

Quick-Roasted Garlic

MAKES 1 HEAD OF GARLIC

1 head of garlic

1 tsp grape seed oil

TIP: Add either of these roasted garlic recipes to dips (such as hummus), dressings, sauces, or anything you want to enhance with a sweet, garlicky flavor.

PREP TIME 5 MIN. | TOTAL TIME 25 MIN.

01 Preheat the oven to 375 degrees F (190 degrees C). Peel apart the garlic cloves, leaving the skin on.

02 Place the garlic cloves on a rimmed baking sheet. Drizzle with a bit of grape seed oil. Bake for 17-23 minutes, or until the garlic is fragrant and slightly browned (this will depend on the size of the garlic cloves). Begin watching closely near the 15-minute mark to ensure that the cloves don't burn.

03 Remove from the oven and set aside. Once cooled, peel away the outside skins and add to a recipe as instructed.

Peanut Sauce

MAKES ¾ CUP

½ cup (128g) salted natural peanut butter (or substitute cashew butter or almond butter)

1½-2 Tbsp (22-30ml) tamari or soy sauce

2-3 Tbsp (24-36g) coconut sugar or organic brown sugar plus more to taste

½ lime, juiced (1 Tbsp or 15ml)

½ tsp chili garlic sauce

2-4 Tbsp (30-60ml) hot water to thin

PREP TIME 5 MIN. | TOTAL TIME 5 MIN.

01 In a small bowl, whisk the peanut butter, tamari, coconut sugar, lime juice, and chili garlic sauce together. Add the hot water to thin until pourable. Taste and adjust the seasonings as needed.

02 Leftovers keep covered in refrigerator for 7-10 days. Add more hot water if the sauce becomes too thick after chilling.

03 Pairs well with dishes like pad Thai, stir-fries, rice noodle salads, spring rolls, and more.

Crispy Baked Tofu

MAKES 2 CUPS

1 14-ounce (396g) package extra-firm tofu

Serving Suggestions

OPTION 01: Stir-fry the tofu in a skillet over medium-high heat in a touch of oil with soy sauce, chili garlic sauce, or store-bought Asian glaze.

OPTION 02: My favorite preparation is marinating tofu in Peanut Sauce (see the recipe above) diluted with 2 Tbsp (30ml) soy sauce, 1 tsp toasted sesame oil, and 1 Tbsp (15ml) maple syrup. Let marinate for 5 minutes, tossing occasionally. Heat a large skillet over medium heat. Once hot, scoop out the tofu with a slotted spoon, leaving most of the sauce behind, and sauté for 5 minutes. Flip/stir occasionally. Remove and serve with the remaining marinade. This is especially delicious over Cauliflower Rice (page 8).

PREP TIME 15 MIN. | TOTAL TIME 45 MIN.

01 Preheat the oven to 400 degrees F (204 degrees C).

02 Drain the tofu. Remove from the package and wrap it in a clean, absorbent towel. Set something heavy on top, such as a cast-iron skillet, to apply pressure.

03 Let the tofu dry for 15 minutes while the oven preheats. Then unwrap and slice the tofu into 1-inch cubes or small rectangles.

04 Arrange the tofu on a parchment paper-lined baking sheet, leaving space between each piece, and bake for a total of 23-35 minutes, flipping once halfway through to ensure even cooking. This will dry out the tofu and give it a firmer texture. Bake for 30-35 minutes for firmer texture, or 23-28 minutes for softer texture.

05 Remove from the oven and let cool while other ingredients are prepared. The tofu is now ready to be added to your recipe.

Quick-Pickled Onions

MAKES 1 CUP

¾ cup (180ml) warm water

½ cup (120ml) red wine vinegar

2 Tbsp (25g) organic cane sugar

½ tsp sea salt

1 small red onion (100g), thinly sliced

PREP TIME 5 MIN. | TOTAL TIME 50 MIN.

01 Add the water, vinegar, sugar, and salt to a mason jar. Shake vigorously to combine until the sugar is dissolved.

02 Add the sliced onion and push down to immerse. Cover with a secure lid and set in the refrigerator for at least 30-45 minutes. Pickled onions will keep covered in the refrigerator for several weeks.

03 These make a great addition to salads, curry dishes, sandwiches, and more. Substitute thinly sliced radishes or carrots for the onion if desired.

Brown Sugar Pecans

MAKES 1 CUP

1 cup (100g) raw pecan halves

2 Tbsp (28g) melted vegan butter or grape seed oil

2 Tbsp (27g) organic brown sugar or coconut sugar

Healthy pinch each of sea salt, ground cinnamon, and cayenne pepper

TIP: These make an excellent addition to my Blender Sweet Potato Pie (page 229), salads, breakfast cereals, and desserts, as well as a quick and easy snack on their own.

PREP TIME 5 MIN. | TOTAL TIME 20 MIN.

01 Preheat the oven to 350 degrees F (176 degrees C). Place the pecans on a foil-lined rimmed baking sheet. Toast for 8 minutes.

02 In the meantime, warm the butter in a small skillet or in the microwave. Stir in the brown sugar, salt, cinnamon, and cayenne.

03 Remove the pecans from the oven. Toss with the spice mixture. Spread back onto the baking sheet and toast for 4-7 minutes more, or until golden brown, being careful not to burn.

04 Remove the pecans from the oven and let them cool slightly. Taste and adjust the seasonings as needed, adding more salt, sugar, or spices as desired.

05 Let cool completely. Store in a well-sealed jar for up to 10 days.

Easy Vegan BBQ Sauce

YIELDS 2¼ CUPS

PREP TIME 5 MIN. | **COOK TIME 20 MIN.**
| **TOTAL TIME 25 MIN.**

2 cups (480g) naturally sweetened ketchup* (organic when possible)

3 Tbsp (45ml) apple cider vinegar

¼ cup (60ml) water

½ lemon, juiced (2 Tbsp or 30ml)

optional: ¼ tsp hot sauce

1 Tbsp (15ml) tamari or soy sauce

1 tsp plain yellow mustard

¼ cup (55g) muscovado sugar or organic brown sugar

3 Tbsp (36g) coconut sugar, plus more to taste

1 tsp onion powder

1 Tbsp (7g) chili powder

2 tsp smoked paprika

⅛ tsp ground cayenne or chipotle pepper, plus more to taste

¼ tsp each sea salt and ground black pepper

01 Add all the ingredients to a large saucepan and whisk thoroughly to combine. Warm over medium heat.

02 Once bubbling, reduce the heat to low and continue simmering for 15 minutes, whisking occasionally.

03 Taste and adjust the seasonings as needed, adding more lemon juice or apple cider vinegar for acidity, muscovado sugar for sweetness, chili powder for smokiness, or cayenne or hot sauce for heat.

04 Let cool completely before transferring to a storage container, such as a large mason jar. Sauce will keep for 3-4 weeks in the refrigerator. Serve at room temperature for best flavor.

Notes

*To keep this sauce gluten-free, use tamari instead of soy sauce.

*The best places to find natural ketchup are Whole Foods, farmers markets, or health food stores in your area.

Methods

I USE SEVERAL PROCESSES AND METHODS FREQUENTLY THROUGHOUT this cookbook, and they are detailed here. Using these methods has greatly improved the quality and precision of my recipes, and I hope the same will be true for you.

In addition, you'll learn how to properly measure ingredients, master my 1-bowl baking technique, and choose the best kitchen equipment for your needs. The more you familiarize yourself with these methods, the easier they will become. But more important, mastering them will ensure that you achieve the best possible results with each recipe.

SOAKING CASHEWS

Several of the recipes in this cookbook require soaking cashews. If this is new to you, don't be intimidated. Unless otherwise noted, measure out raw cashews and place them in a bowl. Top with cool water, cover, and soak for 6-8 hours or overnight at room temperature. Do not exceed 10 hours or the cashews can develop an unsavory flavor. Drain thoroughly and add to a recipe as instructed. If you are not using the cashews until later, drain the cashews, cover them, and put them in the refrigerator for up to 24 hours.

If you forgot to soak your cashews ahead of time, use this quick-soaking method: Measure the cashews, cover them with boiling water, and let them soak, uncovered, for 1 hour. Drain thoroughly and add to a recipe as instructed.

Soaked cashews create a creamy, dairy-free base in dishes such as ice cream, cheesecake, dressings, and pasta sauces.

ALMOND MEAL

Several of the recipes in this cookbook call for almond meal, which I always grind from raw almonds in the bowl of a food processor or high-speed blender until a fine meal is achieved, rather than buying it at the store. I mention this because store-bought almond meal can vary in weight and thus affect the outcome of your recipe. So when you see almond meal listed in a recipe, know that ½ cup = 55 grams (1 Tbsp = 6.8g) for the best accuracy.

SPOON AND LEVEL METHOD

When measuring dry ingredients used in this cookbook, be sure to use the spoon and level method. Use a large spoon to scoop the dry ingredients (such as flour or cocoa powder) into a measuring cup, then use a knife or flat-edged object to scrape off any excess. Do this instead of scooping directly with your measuring implement, which can pack too much of the ingredient into your cup. This method will ensure the most accurate measurements and best results for the recipes.

1-BOWL BAKING TIP

To simplify my baking process and make 1-bowl recipes possible, I often use a handheld sifter or fine-mesh strainer to combine my dry ingredients, and sift them over my wet ingredients. This saves time, means one fewer bowl on the counter, and requires less cleanup. For this reason, I recommend investing in a small sifter or fine-mesh strainer for the 1-bowl recipes in this cookbook. Otherwise, whisk the dry ingredients in a second bowl and add them to the wet ingredients as instructed.

BLENDER TIP

Many of the recipes in this cookbook require a blender to achieve nut meals, smoothies, creamy sauces, and smooth ice creams. To make sure you get the best results, I recommend using a quality high-speed blender, such as a Vitamix, Blendtec, or KitchenAid blender. I recognize this is an investment, but it's well worth it in my opinion, especially for those looking to cook more plant-based recipes. I use my blender every day for smoothies, soups, sauces, and more, and find that a quality machine makes all the difference in achieving the texture I'm looking for.

GINGER COLADA GREEN SMOOTHIE, PAGE 25

Breakfast

FOR ME, NO MEAL TRUMPS BREAKFAST. I FIND THAT WHAT I CHOOSE TO EAT in the morning sets the tone for the rest of the day. Personally, I like my first meal to be substantial and vegetable-heavy, but also accompanied by the occasional sweet something.

I *am* a baker, after all.

This first section is filled with all those things: a few baked goods, a smattering of savory eats, waffles, smoothies, and, of course, pancakes.

Indulge, fuel, be nourished, and start your day off right with these recipes. The Ginger Colada Green Smoothie is one of my absolute favorites. Try it and fall in love. You'll find it difficult *not* to have it every morning. Dig in, friends. It's breakfast time!

SUPER GREEN JUICE 21

HOMEMADE HIPPIE CEREAL 22

GINGER COLADA GREEN SMOOTHIE 25

BEET + GREEN APPLE YOGURT SMOOTHIE 26

SUPER POWERED CHOCOLATE SHAKE 29

DOUBLE CHOCOLATE GLUTEN-FREE WAFFLES 30

MANGO COCONUT LASSI 33

SPICED BUCKWHEAT PANCAKES 34

RUSTIC GARLIC + ASPARAGUS TOFU QUICHE 37

ALMOND BUTTER + JELLY GRANOLA BARS 40

THE VEGAN BREAKFAST BURRITO 43

SAVORY EGGLESS BENEDICT 45

PUMPKIN CHOCOLATE CHIP OAT BREAD 48

1-BOWL ZUCCHINI WALNUT MUFFINS 51

BANANA CHOCOLATE PECAN MUFFINS 53

CARROT WALNUT BREAD 56

EXTRA-BOOZY BERRY MIMOSAS 59

Super Green Juice

I have tried fresh-pressed green juices before, but I could hardly hack the intense, earthy flavor. This recipe is my delicious response. My version is balanced with the addition of apple and banana. Boost the sweetness even more with fresh pineapple. What makes this recipe even better? No juicer required!

SERVES 4

PREP TIME 15 MIN. | **TOTAL TIME 15 MIN.**

2-3 cups (480-720ml) filtered water

1 small handful of parsley (~½ cup or 30g)

1 small handful of cilantro (~½ cup or 30g)

1 small handful of spinach (~½ cup or 30g)

1 small handful of kale (~½ cup or 30g)

2 stalks celery (80g), chopped

1 small knob of fresh ginger, skin removed

1 cucumber (~200g), chopped

1 large sweet apple (~180g), cored and quartered

1 large ripe banana or 1 cup (165g) fresh pineapple

1 lemon, juiced (2 Tbsp or 30ml)

01 Add all of the ingredients to the bowl of a high-speed blender, starting with 2 cups (480ml) water, and add more if the ingredients have trouble blending together. Blend until completely smooth.

02 Taste and adjust the flavors as needed, adding more apple or banana for sweetness, ginger for bite, or lemon for tartness.

03 Drape a large, thin dish towel over a large bowl and pour the juice over, making sure to pour only as much as the towel can comfortably fit (you may have to pour in batches).

04 Carefully gather the corners of the towel and lift up, then twist and squeeze out as much juice as possible, leaving the pulp behind in the towel. Use the pulp in baked goods, smoothies, or compost.

05 Serve immediately, or chill for 1-2 hours in the refrigerator. The juice will keep for at least 2 days covered in the refrigerator, though the best flavor and nutrient payoff are when the juice is fresh.

Homemade Hippie Cereal

Any time I make my own cereal and granola I feel like a flower child, hence the name of this recipe. This cereal is inspired by my Grain-Free Granola on the blog, but this version requires just 10 ingredients and boasts way more volume. Top with banana and dairy-free milk for a healthy, hearty, simple breakfast.

YIELDS 21 SERVINGS

| PREP TIME 10 MIN. | COOK TIME 25 MIN. | TOTAL TIME 35 MIN. |

1¼ cups (196g) slivered raw almonds (slivered do better than whole)

1¼ cups (125g) raw pecans

¾ cup (90g) raw walnuts

2 Tbsp (24g) chia seeds

2 tsp ground cinnamon

2 Tbsp (24g) coconut sugar (or substitute organic cane sugar, or organic muscovado sugar)

¼ tsp sea salt

2 Tbsp (30ml) olive oil or coconut oil

¼ cup (60ml) maple syrup or agave nectar

6 cups (84g) puffed brown rice cereal

OPTIONAL

¼ cup (28g) roasted unsalted sunflower seeds

¼ cup (35g) dried blueberries or other dried fruit

TIP: If you have trouble finding puffed rice, substitute another puffed cereal or omit and enjoy as a granola.

01 Preheat the oven to 325 degrees F (162 degrees C). Position a rack in the center of the oven.

02 In a large bowl, combine the almonds, pecans, walnuts, chia, 1 tsp cinnamon, coconut sugar, and salt.

03 In a small saucepan over low heat (or in a small bowl in the microwave), warm the olive oil and maple syrup. Pour over the dry ingredients in the large bowl. Mix well.

04 Spread the mixture evenly onto a large rimmed baking sheet. Bake for 20 minutes. If adding the sunflower seeds and dried fruit, remove the baking sheet from the oven and add at this time. Stir.

05 Raise the oven temperature to 340 degrees F (171 degrees C) and return the baking sheet to the oven for another 5-7 minutes, or until deep golden brown.

06 Rinse and dry the bowl. As soon as the granola is visibly browned and done cooking, about 25 minutes total, remove from the oven and let cool completely.

07 When completely cooled, pour the puffed rice into the bowl and add remaining 1 tsp cinnamon. Toss. Add the cooled granola and toss once more.

08 Store in a container with an airtight seal. The cereal will keep 2-3 weeks. Serve as is or with dairy-free yogurt or milk. Sliced banana makes a lovely addition.

Ginger Colada Green Smoothie

This is my absolute favorite recipe of the breakfast bunch, and one that I make almost every morning. Loaded with nutritious ingredients like fresh ginger, kale, spinach, and hemp seeds, this is the perfect way to jump-start your day. I call it a ginger colada because it reminds me of a piña colada with a gingery kick.

SERVES 2

PREP TIME 10 MIN. | **TOTAL TIME 10 MIN.**

1 Tbsp fresh ginger (~1 small knob, skin removed)

½ lemon or lime, juiced (1 Tbsp or 15ml)

⅓ cup (78ml) light coconut milk

1½ cups (210g) chopped frozen pineapple

1 small banana, peeled, sliced, and frozen

1 large handful of spinach*

1 small handful of kale*

⅔ cup (160ml) unsweetened plain almond milk or DIY Almond Milk (page 6)

¾ cup (180ml) filtered water

OPTIONAL

1 Tbsp (7g) flaxseed meal

1 Tbsp (10g) raw hulled hemp seeds

1 Tbsp (15ml) maple syrup or agave nectar (depending on the sweetness of the banana/pineapple)

01 Add all of the ingredients to the bowl of a blender in the order listed, and blend thoroughly on high speed until completely smooth. If it isn't quite blending, add a bit more water or almond milk.

02 Let blend for a good 2-3 minutes on high so everything gets very well blended together, especially the ginger.

03 Taste and adjust seasonings as needed, adding more frozen banana or sweetener of choice for added sweetness, lime juice for acidity, or coconut milk for creaminess.

04 Serve immediately. Store leftovers covered in the refrigerator for up to 24 hours, though it's best when fresh.

Note

*I like to buy my spinach and kale prewashed and bagged and keep it in the freezer so it stays fresh and is always available when I am craving a smoothie. It also helps keep the smoothie colder and slightly creamier.

Beet + Green Apple Yogurt Smoothie

Beets? In a smoothie? Yes! And I promise you will be surprised at how the yogurt and berries work together to mask the intense earthiness of this gorgeous root vegetable. Loaded with tons of vitamins and nutrients, this vibrant smoothie has become an unexpected breakfast favorite for me.

SERVES 2

PREP TIME 10 MIN. | **TOTAL TIME 10 MIN.**

1 green apple (250g), cored and quartered (weighed whole)

1 small red beet (82g), skin removed, quartered*

1¼ cups (320g) soy or coconut vanilla yogurt (if plain, add vanilla extract and sweetener of choice)*

½ cup (60g) mixed frozen berries

¼ cup (60ml) unsweetened almond milk, DIY Almond Milk (page 6), or orange juice

½ lime, juiced (1 Tbsp or 15ml)

01 Add all of the ingredients to the bowl of a blender and blend on high until creamy and smooth, typically 1-2 minutes.

02 Taste and adjust the flavor as needed, adding more berries for sweetness, lime for acidity, yogurt for creaminess, or a few ice cubes to thicken and chill.

03 Divide between two glasses and serve immediately. Best when fresh.

Notes

*If you're beet-averse, I would suggest swapping out the beet for an extra ½ cup (60g) berries.

*If you can't find dairy-free yogurt, omit it and substitute 1 small frozen banana and ¼ cup (60ml) more almond milk.

Super Powered Chocolate Shake

Everyone needs a breakfast shake in their recipe arsenal. This one is mine. Creamy, chocolaty, loaded with nutrients, this shake is great for workout recovery or when you are craving something sweet and guilt-free.

SERVES 2

PREP TIME 10 MIN. | **TOTAL TIME 10 MIN.**

1½ cups (360ml) unsweetened plain almond milk or DIY Almond Milk (page 6)

2 Tbsp (12g) cacao powder or unsweetened cocoa powder

1 Tbsp (16g) salted almond butter (if unsalted, add a pinch of salt)

1½ tsp chia seeds

1½ tsp flaxseeds

1 ripe banana, peeled, sliced, and frozen

2-4 ice cubes

OPTIONAL
1 date, pitted (depending on ripeness of the banana)

01 Add all of the ingredients to the bowl of a blender. Blend until creamy and smooth, scraping down the sides as needed. Add more almond milk to thin, or more ice to thicken.

02 Taste and adjust the flavors as needed, adding more cacao powder for a more intense chocolate flavor, more sliced banana or dates for sweetness, or more almond butter for creaminess.

03 Serves 1 generously or 2 modestly. You can keep leftovers covered in the refrigerator for 24-48 hours, though it's best when fresh.

Double Chocolate Gluten-Free Waffles

Everyone loves chocolate. Everyone loves waffles. You put the two together and what you get is magical. These gluten-free wonders are crisp on the outside, tender on the inside, and insanely delicious. Serve with fresh fruit or a generous drizzle of nut butter for a substantial breakfast or snack. They are delicious fresh, or easily reheated from the freezer in the toaster or oven.

YIELDS 5 LARGE WAFFLES

PREP TIME 20 MIN. | **COOK TIME 10 MIN.** | **TOTAL TIME 30 MIN.**

1½ cups (360ml) unsweetened plain almond milk or DIY Almond Milk (page 6)

1 tsp apple cider vinegar or lemon juice

¼ cup (60ml) melted coconut oil or melted vegan butter

1½ tsp pure vanilla extract

2 Tbsp (30ml) maple syrup or agave nectar

⅓ cup plus 1 Tbsp (37g) unsweetened cocoa powder

1½ cups (240g) Gluten-Free Flour Blend (page 7)

½ cup (45g) gluten-free rolled oats

1 Tbsp (7g) flaxseed meal

¼ tsp sea salt

1½ tsp baking powder

2 Tbsp (25g) organic cane sugar

OPTIONAL
⅓ cup (60g) vegan chocolate chips, plus more for topping

01 Combine the almond milk and vinegar in a medium bowl and let set for 5 minutes to curdle.

02 Add the coconut oil, vanilla, and maple syrup and whisk. Set aside.

03 In a separate medium bowl, add the cocoa powder, flour blend, oats, flaxseed meal, salt, baking powder, and sugar and whisk until well combined.

04 Add the wet ingredients to the dry ingredients. Mix until well incorporated. Then add the chocolate chips, if using, and stir once more. If the batter appears too thick, thin it with a bit more almond milk.

05 Let the batter rest for 10 minutes while waffle iron preheats. (Mine has a scale of 1-5, and I set it at 4 for crispier waffles, but adjust yours according to preference.)

06 Once the waffle iron is ready, generously coat it with nonstick spray or vegan butter, and scoop on about ⅓ cup batter, or whatever amount covers the surface.

07 Cook according to the manufacturer's instructions and to desired crispiness.

08 Serve with desired toppings, such as cocoa powder, vegan butter, Coconut Whipped Cream (page 8), or fresh berries.

09 Store leftovers in a freezer-safe bag or container, and reheat in the toaster for best results. Waffles will keep in a freezer for 1-2 months, though they're freshest within the first 2 weeks.

TIP: Place waffles on a baking rack in a 200 degree F (93 degree C) oven to keep warm. Keep waffles in a single layer to ensure crispiness—stacking can cause sogginess.

Mango Coconut Lassi

Mango lovers, rejoice! This creamy, smoothie-like beverage gets its creamy texture from coconut cream, coconut yogurt, and gorgeous, ripe mangoes. Fresh lime juice and a pinch of cardamom inject brightness and warmth. Enjoy this for breakfast, as a snack, or alongside your favorite Indian dishes.

SERVES 2

PREP TIME 5 MIN. | **TOTAL TIME 5 MIN.**

6 ounces (170g) plain or vanilla coconut yogurt or other yogurt of choice

2 small ripe mangoes, cubed (~2 cups or 300g)

2 Tbsp (30ml) coconut cream (or substitute full-fat coconut milk)

2-3 Tbsp (30-45ml) unsweetened plain almond milk or DIY Almond Milk (page 6)

⅛-¼ tsp cardamom, to taste

1-2 Tbsp (15-30ml) maple syrup or coconut sugar (depending on the sweetness of the yogurt/mango)

OPTIONAL
¼ cup (35g) ice cubes (for colder drink)

1 sprig of fresh mint, for garnish

01 Add all of the ingredients to the bowl of a blender and blend until creamy and smooth. Add more almond milk if the ingredients aren't blending together well.

02 Taste and adjust the flavor as needed, then divide between two glasses, garnish with mint (optional), and serve.

03 Store the leftovers covered in the refrigerator for up to 2 days (or freeze into popsicles). Best when fresh.

Spiced Buckwheat Pancakes

Dare I say these are my favorite vegan pancakes to date? Besides my Chocolate Chip Oatmeal Cookie Pancakes—my very first recipe on the blog—these contend for top choice! These hearty, wholesome pancakes are warmed with cardamom, cinnamon, and ginger, and they get a sweet kick from molasses and maple syrup. Tender and perfectly sweet, they make the perfect breakfast on a chilly fall or winter morning.

MAKES 8 PANCAKES

PREP TIME 15 MIN.	COOK TIME 10 MIN.	TOTAL TIME 25 MIN.

1 Flax Egg (page 6)

1 Tbsp (15ml) olive oil, grape seed oil, or melted coconut oil, plus more for oiling the griddle

1 Tbsp (15ml) maple syrup

1 Tbsp (20g) blackstrap molasses*

½ tsp baking soda

1½ tsp baking powder

⅛ tsp cardamom

½ tsp ground cinnamon

¼ tsp ground ginger

Pinch of sea salt

1 cup plus 1 Tbsp (255ml) unsweetened plain almond milk or DIY Almond Milk (page 6)

¼ cup (30g) buckwheat flour

¾ cup (90g) spelt flour, whole wheat pastry flour, or unbleached all-purpose flour

2 Tbsp (22g) rolled oats

01 Prepare the flax egg in a large bowl. Let sit for 5 minutes.

02 Add the olive oil, maple syrup, molasses, baking soda, baking powder, cardamom, cinnamon, ginger, and salt. Whisk to combine.

03 Add the almond milk and whisk until combined.

04 Next, add buckwheat flour, spelt flour, and oats. Stir until just combined, being careful not to overmix. If the batter looks too thick, thin with a little more almond milk. It should be semi-thick but pourable. Taste and adjust spices/sweetness as needed.

05 Let the batter rest 5 minutes while preheating an electric griddle or skillet to medium heat (or about 325 degrees F/162 degrees C). The surface should be hot but not screaming hot–the oil shouldn't smoke when it makes contact with the surface.

06 Lightly grease the griddle with oil of your choice and pour ¼ cup measurements of batter onto the griddle.

07 Flip when bubbles appear in the middle of the pancakes and the edges appear slightly dry. Be careful not to burn the pancakes.

continued

08 Cook for 1-2 minutes more, then serve. Top with vegan butter and a drizzle of maple syrup or other desired toppings. Fruit compote is also delicious.

09 Leftovers reheat well in the microwave or a 350 degree F (176 degree C) oven. Otherwise, freeze the cooked pancakes in a single layer on a rimmed baking sheet. Once frozen, transfer to a freezer-safe container or plastic bag. Reheat in the toaster, oven, or microwave.

Note

*If you do not have molasses, replace with 1 extra Tbsp (15ml) maple syrup or 1 Tbsp (12g) coconut sugar.

Rustic Garlic + Asparagus Tofu Quiche

If you've never tried making a tofu quiche, it's time. This gluten-free version is light in texture, loaded with protein, and gets tons of flavor from garlic and asparagus. Keep it seasonal with vegetables you have on hand. This is the perfect brunch item and is especially great for picnics and baby or bridal showers since it's delicious served hot or at room temperature.

SERVES 6

PREP TIME 45 MIN.	COOK TIME 55 MIN.	TOTAL TIME 1 HR. 40 MIN.

CRUST

1¼ cup (200g) Gluten-Free Flour Blend (page 7)

¼ tsp sea salt

6 Tbsp (84g) cold vegan butter

3-7 Tbsp (45-105ml) ice-cold water

FILLING

12 ounces (340g) extra-firm silken tofu, patted dry*

2 Tbsp (6g) nutritional yeast

3 Tbsp (45g) plain hummus

1 Tbsp (7g) cornstarch or arrowroot starch

2 Tbsp (30ml) olive oil, plus more for brushing on top

Sea salt and black pepper

1 bundle asparagus (~2 cups or 268g)

4 cloves garlic (2 Tbsp or 12g), minced

01 To prepare the crust, add the flour and salt to a large bowl. Whisk to combine.

02 Slice or dollop the cold butter into the mixture and work gently with a fork or pastry cutter to cut it in. When it's done, the mixture should resemble wet sand.

03 Add ice-cold water 1 Tbsp (15ml) at a time, and use a wooden spoon to stir. Only add as much water as needed to help the dough come together.

04 When a loose dough has formed, transfer it to a piece of plastic wrap. Gently form into a ½-inch-thick disc. Wrap firmly and refrigerate for a minimum of 30 minutes, and up to 2 days.

05 Once the dough is chilled, preheat the oven to 375 degrees F (190 degrees C) and prepare the filling.

06 To roll out the crust, remove the dough from the refrigerator and let it warm for up to 5 minutes before using. It should not be too warm, or it can become too soft to handle. Unwrap the disc and place between two sizable layers of wax paper or parchment paper. Using a rolling pin, gently roll the crust into a circle slightly larger than the pie pan (mine is

continued

9½ inches or 24cm). If it cracks, don't stress you can re-form it with your hands once you get it in the pan. But try to be gentle.

07 To transfer the crust, remove the top layer of wax paper, and gently lay the pie dish facedown on top of the crust. Use the support of the wax paper to quickly but carefully invert it.

08 Once the crust is inverted, gently use your hands to form it into the pan, working the crust up along the sides. Just try not to overwork the dough in the process—it should not take more than a few minutes to perfect the shape. Any holes or cracks can be mended with a little excess dough and the heat of your hand.

09 To prepare the tofu filling, add the drained tofu to the bowl of a food processor, along with the nutritional yeast, hummus, cornstarch, 1 Tbsp (15ml) olive oil, and about ¼ tsp each salt and pepper. Purée until creamy and smooth. Set aside.

10 Heat a large skillet over medium heat. In the meantime, prepare the asparagus by setting aside 8-12 whole spears (for topping quiche) and chopping the rest into 1-inch pieces.

11 Once the skillet is hot, add the remaining 1 Tbsp (15ml) olive oil, chopped asparagus, garlic, and a healthy pinch of salt and pepper. Toss to coat. Sauté for 3-4 minutes, or until fragrant and just softened.

12 Add the sautéed garlic and asparagus to the filling and stir. Spread the mixture onto the prepared crust and smooth into an even layer. Add the whole asparagus spears on top of quiche and gently press to adhere. Then brush the asparagus with a bit of olive oil to encourage browning.

13 Bake the quiche for 40-50 minutes, or until the top appears golden brown and firm. If the crust begins to get too brown, cover the edges with foil by crimping pieces of foil around the edges of the crust, leaving the center of the pie bare.

14 Let cool at least 15 minutes before serving. Store leftovers loosely covered in the fridge for up to 2 days, though quiche is best when fresh.

Notes

*I often use Bob's Red Mill Gluten Free 1-to-1 Baking Flour in my piecrusts, as I love its finely milled texture. However, if you cannot find it at the store, my Gluten-Free Flour Blend (page 7) works great as well.

*If you are not gluten-free, you can substitute unbleached all-purpose flour for the gluten-free flour.

*Be sure to use silken tofu for best results.

Almond Butter + Jelly Granola Bars

This recipe is a spin on my 5-Ingredient Granola Bars from the blog, infused with creamy almond butter and dried strawberries. The flavor is reminiscent of a PB&J sandwich but boasts more protein, fiber, and no gluten, making these a healthier option the whole family will love.

MAKES 10 BARS

PREP TIME 15 MIN.* | **COOK TIME 15 MIN.** | **TOTAL TIME 30 MIN.**

1½ cups (135g) rolled oats (gluten-free for GF eaters)

¾ cup (84g) raw almonds, walnuts, or pecans, chopped

1 heaping cup packed (~220g) dates, pitted (Deglet Nour or Medjool)*

¼ cup (60ml) maple syrup or agave nectar

¼ cup (64g) creamy salted natural almond butter (or substitute peanut or sunflower butter)

⅓ cup (43g) dried strawberries, coarsely chopped (or substitute dried blueberries, cherries, apricots, etc.)

01 Preheat the oven to 350 degrees F (176 degrees C).

02 Add the oats and almonds to a rimmed baking sheet and bake for 11-13 minutes, or until slightly golden brown. Set aside.

03 In the meantime, add the dates to the bowl of a blender or food processor. Blend until small bits remain, about 1 minute. A dough-like consistency should form. (Mine rolls into a ball.)

04 Place the toasted oats, almonds, and dates in a large bowl.

05 Warm the maple syrup and nut butter in a small saucepan over low heat for 2-3 minutes. Stir and pour over the oat mixture. Mix, breaking up the dates to disperse throughout. Use a spoon or your hands to thoroughly mix.

06 Add the dried strawberries and stir once more to combine.

07 Transfer to an 8 × 8-inch dish or other small pan lined with plastic wrap or parchment paper to facilitate removal.

08 Cover with parchment paper or plastic wrap. Press down with something flat, such as a book, to pack tightly. Chill in the freezer for 15-20 minutes to harden.

09 Remove the bars from the dish and cut into 10 even bars. Store in an airtight container for 5-7 days, or in the freezer for 1 month.

Notes

*If the dates are dried out, soak in warm water for 10 minutes, then drain well.

*Prep time does not include chilling the bars.

The Vegan Breakfast Burrito

Our cookbook designer, Holly, pleaded that I add this recipe to the cookbook as it was sure to be a crowd-pleaser. She was right. The original inspiration was difficult to tackle while keeping within my simple standards, so I made a few adjustments and came up with something amazing. I would be proud to serve this to meat-lovers and plant–based folks alike. It is hearty, filling, and versatile. Multiply the recipe to serve more, and serve it buffet style to let everyone build their own dream burrito.

SERVES 2

| PREP TIME 15 MIN. | COOK TIME 15 MIN. | TOTAL TIME 30 MIN. |

RICE
¾ cup (150g) white rice, rinsed and drained

1½ cups (360ml) water

¼ tsp sea salt

½ lime, juiced (1 Tbsp or 15ml)

¼ cup (15g) fresh cilantro, chopped

HASH BROWNS + ONIONS
4 small red potatoes*

½ red onion (55g)

1-2 Tbsp (14-28g) vegan butter (or 15-30ml olive oil)

¼ tsp each sea salt and black pepper

BLACK BEANS
1 cup (185g) cooked black beans (if unsalted, add ¼ tsp salt)

¼ tsp each ground cumin, garlic powder, and chili powder

continued

01 Start by adding the rice, water, and salt to a saucepan and bringing it to a boil. Once boiling, reduce the heat to low, cover, and simmer for 15-20 minutes or until all of the water is absorbed and the rice is fluffy. Remove from the heat and set aside.

02 As the rice is cooking, heat a large metal or cast-iron skillet over medium heat. Wash and chop potatoes into bite-size pieces.* Slice the onion into ¼-inch rings.

03 Once the skillet is hot, add the vegan butter. Swirl to coat. Add the potatoes to one half of the pan and the onions to the remaining half. Season with the salt and pepper, cover, and let cook for 4-5 minutes on one side. Then flip/toss to brown on the other side for 4-5 minutes, or until golden brown. Remove from the heat and set aside.

04 Add the beans to a small saucepan over medium heat and season with the cumin, garlic power, and chili powder. When bubbly, reduce the heat to low to keep warm.

05 To make the slaw, mash together the avocado and lime juice, then add the cabbage and jalapeño and toss to combine. Season with a pinch of salt and set aside.

continued

QUICK AVOCADO SLAW
¼ ripe avocado

1 lime, juiced
(2 Tbsp or 30ml)

1 cup (89g) purple
cabbage, green cabbage,
or radish, thinly sliced

1 (14g) jalapeño, seeds
removed, thinly sliced

Pinch each of sea salt
and black pepper

FOR SERVING
2 large vegan flour
tortillas (white
or wheat, to your
preference)

½ ripe avocado, sliced

¼ cup (64g) salsa

OPTIONAL
Hot sauce

06 To the cooked rice, add the lime juice
and cilantro. Toss with a fork to combine.

07 To soften the tortillas, wrap in a
damp towel and warm in the microwave for
30 seconds, or in a 350 degree F oven
(176 degrees C) for 1-2 minutes.

08 Add the fillings in any order, followed
by sliced avocado and salsa (or hot sauce,
if desired). Roll up, slice in half, and
enjoy. Serve any extra potatoes, black
beans, or rice on the side.

Note

*This recipe yields leftover potatoes, rice, and
black beans, all of which are calculated into
the nutrition information (page 282). Specific
nutrition information will vary depending how
generously you fill your burrito.

Savory Eggless Benedict

After going dairy-free, I mourned the loss of eggs Benedict. But this plant-based version satisfies the craving! If you are a fan of creamy sauces and avocado toast, this is the dish for you. Toasted English muffins, sautéed tomatoes, and ripe avocados are topped with a seriously decadent vegan hollandaise that gives the real thing a run for its money.

SERVES 2
SAUCE YIELDS 8 SERVINGS

| PREP TIME 10 MIN. | COOK TIME 20 MIN. | TOTAL TIME 30 MIN. |

HOLLANDAISE

2 Tbsp (30ml) grape seed oil, avocado oil, or melted coconut oil

4 cloves garlic (2 Tbsp or 12g), minced

1¼ Tbsp (15g) unbleached all-purpose flour or arrowroot starch

1½-1¾ cups (360-420ml) unsweetened plain almond milk or DIY Almond Milk (page 6)

⅓ cup (80ml) vegetable broth

½ lemon, juiced (1 Tbsp or 15ml), plus more to taste

1-2 Tbsp (36g) nutritional yeast

Pinch each of sea salt and black pepper, plus more to taste

1 Tbsp (15ml) maple syrup or agave nectar

OPTIONAL

1 Tbsp (14g) tahini

½-1 tsp hot sauce

continued

01 To make the hollandaise, heat a large skillet over medium heat. Once hot, add the grape seed oil and garlic. Sauté for 1-2 minutes, or until very light golden brown.

02 Add the flour. Whisk to combine. Cook for 1 minute.

03 Slowly add the almond milk and broth, whisking to prevent clumps.

04 Add the lemon, tahini (optional), nutritional yeast, salt, pepper, maple syrup, and hot sauce (optional). Whisk to combine and continue cooking over medium heat to thicken.

05 Transfer the mixture to the bowl of a blender (optional, as blending makes it creamier, but is not vital to the final product) and blend until creamy and smooth. Taste and adjust the seasonings as needed. Return the sauce to the pan over low heat to keep warm.

06 If the sauce is too thin, scoop out ½ cup and whisk in an additional 2-3 tsp flour. Then whisk back into the sauce and continue cooking over medium-low heat until thickened. Repeat the process as needed.

continued

TOMATO + AVOCADO BENEDICT

1 Tbsp (15ml) olive oil

1 ripe tomato, cut into
½-inch-thick slices

Pinch each of sea salt
and black pepper

2 English muffins
(check package for
vegan friendliness)

1 ripe avocado,
thinly sliced

OPTIONAL

¼ red onion, sliced

Smoked paprika and/or
fresh herbs, for garnish

07 As the sauce is cooking, heat a large skillet over medium heat. Once hot, add the olive oil and tomato slices and season with the salt and pepper. Brown for 2 minutes on each side. Set aside.

08 Remove the tomatoes from the skillet and add the English muffins cut-side down to slightly warm/brown for 2-3 minutes.

09 To serve, top the English muffins with the tomato slices, avocado, and a generous portion of hollandaise sauce. Garnish with red onion, paprika, or parsley for color (optional).

10 Store leftover hollandaise sauce covered in the refrigerator for 7-10 days. Reheat in a microwave or small saucepan over medium heat until warmed through.

Pumpkin Chocolate Chip Oat Bread

This bread is a spin-off of my Gluten-Free Pumpkin Bread from the blog that took me years to perfect! I've adapted this version from the original with a few modifications. I also injected a bit of decadence with dark chocolate chips. Enjoy this tender, super-moist, chocolaty bread for breakfast, a snack, or a late-night dessert in the fall.

SERVES 10	PREP TIME 15 MIN.	COOK TIME 45 MIN.	TOTAL TIME 60 MIN.

1½ Flax Eggs (see Flax Egg, page 6)

¾ cup (150g) pumpkin purée

2 Tbsp (32g) ripe banana, mashed (for binding)

¼ cup (60ml) maple syrup or agave nectar

¼ cup (60ml) olive oil, grape seed oil, or melted coconut oil

⅔ cup (147g) organic brown sugar, packed

½ tsp sea salt

2 tsp baking soda

½ tsp ground cinnamon

1 tsp pumpkin pie spice

½ cup (120ml) water

¾ tsp apple cider vinegar or lemon juice

1 cup plus 1 Tbsp (96g) gluten-free rolled oats

½ cup plus 1 Tbsp (62g) almond meal

1¼ cup (200g) Gluten-Free Flour Blend* (page 7)

⅔ cup (120g) vegan dark chocolate chips

01 Prepare the flax eggs in a large bowl and preheat oven to 375 degrees F (190 degrees C).

02 Prepare a 9 × 5-inch loaf pan by lightly greasing or lining with parchment paper.

03 Add the pumpkin purée, banana, maple syrup, and olive oil to the flax eggs. Whisk to combine.

04 Add the brown sugar, salt, baking soda, cinnamon, and pumpkin pie spice. Whisk to combine.

05 Add the water and vinegar. Whisk again.

06 Add the oats, almond meal, and flour. Stir. The batter should be semi-thick but pourable.

07 Add in half of the chocolate chips and stir. Scoop into the prepared loaf pan and top with the remaining chocolate chips.

08 Bake for 43-50 minutes, or until deep golden brown and a toothpick inserted into the center comes out clean.

09 Remove from the oven and let rest in the pan for 15 minutes. Loosen the sides with a butter knife and gently transfer to a plate to cool. Let cool completely,

preferably several hours, before slicing. If cut too early, the bread will be crumbly. Slice gently, as it's rather tender. It's even better the next day (if you can wait).

10 Once cooled, store in a covered container or cover with plastic wrap at room temperature to keep fresh. Freeze for up to 1 month.

Note

*If not gluten-free, substitute whole wheat pastry or unbleached all-purpose flour for the Gluten-Free Flour Blend.

1-Bowl Zucchini Walnut Muffins

These muffins are a different take on my Gluten-Free Zucchini Cake from the blog, with less refined sugar, no eggs, and the addition of walnuts for healthy fats and protein! These hearty, moist-yet-tender muffins are perfect as a take-along breakfast or snack.

MAKES 12 MUFFINS

PREP TIME 20 MIN. | **COOK TIME 35 MIN.** | **TOTAL TIME 55 MIN.**

1½ Flax Eggs (see Flax Egg, page 6)

1 heaping cup (~220g) packed grated zucchini

⅓ cup (87g) very ripe banana, mashed

¼ cup (60ml) olive oil, grape seed oil, or melted coconut oil

¼ cup (60ml) maple syrup or agave nectar

½ cup (123g) unsweetened applesauce or 1 sweet apple, finely grated

½ cup (110g) organic brown sugar, packed

½ tsp sea salt

1½ tsp baking soda

½ tsp ground cinnamon

½ cup (120ml) unsweetened plain almond milk or DIY Almond Milk (page 6)

⅔ cup (60g) gluten-free rolled oats

½ cup (55g) almond meal

1 cup plus 2 Tbsp (180g) Gluten-Free Flour Blend (page 7)

OPTIONAL
¼ cup (30g) raw walnuts, chopped

01 Prepare the flax eggs in a large bowl. Let sit for 5 minutes.

02 Preheat the oven to 375 degrees F (190 degrees C). Lightly grease a standard-size muffin tin or add paper liners.

03 In the meantime, grate the zucchini. Transfer to a clean towel and squeeze out the extra moisture. Set aside.

04 Add the banana to the flax eggs. Mash them together.

05 Add the olive oil and maple syrup. Whisk to combine. Add the applesauce, brown sugar, salt, baking soda, and cinnamon. Whisk to combine.

06 Add the almond milk and grated zucchini. Whisk to combine.

07 Add the gluten-free oats, almond meal, and flour. Stir until just combined.

08 Divide the batter evenly among 12 muffin tins, filling all the way to the top (there may be some leftover batter), and top with chopped walnuts (optional).

09 Bake the muffins for 32-36 minutes, or until deep golden brown and a toothpick inserted into the center comes out clean.*

continued

10 Remove from the oven and let sit in the muffin tin for 10-15 minutes. Transfer to a cooling rack to cool completely.

11 If unwrapped too quickly, the muffins will stick to the liners. Let cool completely before sampling.

12 Once cooled, store in a covered container or plastic bag at room temperature to keep fresh for up to 3 days. Freeze for longer storage.

Note

*If baking in a 9 × 5-inch loaf pan or an 8 × 8-inch cake pan, bake for 45 minutes and check every 5 minutes thereafter for doneness.

Banana Chocolate Pecan Muffins

I don't know if this recipe could be any more perfect in terms of flavor combination. Dark chocolate, ripe banana, and pecans meld together perfectly to create these decadent, rich, and surprisingly healthy muffins. Perfect for a lazy weekend breakfast or take-along snack.

MAKES 11 MUFFINS | **PREP TIME 15 MIN.** | **COOK TIME 20 MIN.** | **TOTAL TIME 35 MIN.**

2 Flax Eggs (See Flax Egg, page 6)

4 medium ripe bananas (1¾ cups or 435g)

2 tsp baking soda

¼ cup plus 1 Tbsp (68g) organic brown sugar, packed

¼ cup (60ml) maple syrup or agave nectar

½ tsp ground cinnamon

½ tsp sea salt

1 tsp pure vanilla extract

¼ cup (60ml) melted coconut oil or melted vegan butter

1 cup (160g) Gluten-Free Flour Blend* (page 7)

½ cup (55g) almond meal

½ cup (45g) gluten-free rolled oats

⅓ cup (33g) raw pecans

⅓ cup (40g) vegan dark chocolate (70% cacao or higher is best), coarsely chopped, plus more for topping

continued

01 Preheat the oven to 375 degrees F (190 degrees C). Lightly grease a standard-size muffin tin or add paper liners.

02 Prepare the flax eggs in a large bowl. Let sit for 5 minutes.

03 Add the banana and baking soda and mash together.

04 Add the brown sugar, maple syrup, cinnamon, and salt. Whisk for 1 minute.

05 Add the vanilla and coconut oil. Whisk again.

06 Add the flour, almond meal, and oats. Stir with a wooden spoon until just combined. Fold in the chocolate.

07 Divide the batter evenly among muffin tins, filling practically full. Top with the pecans and a few sprinkles of chocolate, as well as a little coconut sugar (optional), if using, for a crusty top.

08 Bake for 17-22 minutes or until the tops are golden brown and a toothpick comes out clean.

09 Let cool for 5 minutes in the muffin tin, then gently remove and let cool completely on a cooling rack.

continued

OPTIONAL
1 Tbsp (12g) coconut
sugar or organic cane
sugar, for topping

10 Once cooled, store in a covered
container at room temperature for 3-4 days,
or in the freezer for up to 1 month.

Note

*If you are not gluten-free, substitute whole
wheat pastry flour or unbleached all-purpose
flour for the gluten-free blend.

Carrot Walnut Bread

This 1–bowl quick bread is naturally sweetened, loaded with carrots and rolled oats, and is insanely moist and hearty. It makes the perfect quick snack or light breakfast.

SERVES 10	PREP TIME 15 MIN.	COOK TIME 55 MIN.	TOTAL TIME 1 HR. 10 MIN.

1½ Flax Eggs (see Flax Egg, page 6)

⅓ cup (87g) very ripe banana, mashed

¼ cup (60ml) olive oil

¼ cup plus 1 Tbsp (75ml) maple syrup or agave nectar

½ cup (123g) unsweetened applesauce

⅓ cup (64g) coconut sugar or organic brown sugar

½ tsp sea salt

1½ tsp baking soda

½ tsp baking powder

½ tsp ground cinnamon

½ cup (120ml) unsweetened plain almond milk or DIY Almond Milk (page 6)

1⅛ cups (144g) finely grated carrot

⅔ cup (60g) gluten-free rolled oats

½ cup (55g) almond meal

1 cup plus 2 Tbsp (180g) Gluten-Free Flour Blend* (page 7)

⅓ cup (40g) raw walnuts, chopped, for topping

01 Preheat the oven to 350 degrees F (176 degrees C). Prepare the flax eggs in a large bowl. Lightly grease a 9 x 5-inch loaf pan or line with parchment paper.

02 Add the banana, olive oil, and maple syrup to the flax eggs. Whisk to combine.

03 Add the applesauce, coconut sugar, salt, baking soda, baking powder, and cinnamon. Whisk to combine.

04 Add the almond milk and stir. Add the grated carrot and stir.

05 Add the oats, almond meal, and flour. Whisk until just combined.

06 Spread the batter into the loaf pan and top with the walnuts.

07 Bake for 50-65 minutes, or until deep golden brown and a toothpick inserted into the center comes out completely clean. When pressed on the top, it should not feel too spongy, so do not be afraid of overbaking! The gluten-free blend takes a bit longer than gluten flours to bake.

08 Remove from the oven and rest in the pan for 15 minutes. Then gently transfer the loaf to a cooling rack or plate to cool completely.

09 If you slice it too soon, it may be too tender, as it's a very moist loaf. So it's best to let it cool completely. If you are one of those crazy people with self-control, it's even better the next day.

10 Once cooled, store in a covered container or plastic bag at room temperature to keep fresh for 3-5 days. Freeze for longer storage.

Note

*If not gluten-free, substitute Gluten-Free Flour Blend with an equal amount of unbleached all-purpose flour, spelt flour, or whole wheat pastry flour.

Extra-Boozy Berry Mimosas

Looking for a fabulous way to kick off your weekend activities? This classic mimosa gets some extra flare from orange liqueur and a beautiful dose of color from generous handfuls of summer berries. Hello, fancy weekend!

SERVES 1

PREP TIME 5 MIN. | **TOTAL TIME 5 MIN.**

4 ounces (118ml) dry champagne or sparkling white wine, chilled

½ ounce (~15ml) orange liqueur (such as Grand Marnier, Patron Citronge, or triple sec)

4 ounces (118ml) freshly squeezed orange juice, chilled

¼ cup (30g) mixed berries

01 Add the champagne, orange liqueur, and orange juice to a champagne flute or wineglass and top with the berries. Serve immediately, preferably with good company.

Note

*This can also be prepared in a pitcher by combining 1 bottle (25oz or 750ml) dry champagne, 25oz (750ml) orange juice, ⅓ cup (91ml) orange liqueur, and 1 cup berries. Gently stir to combine. Serves 6.

BALSAMIC + POMEGRANATE ROASTED
SWEET POTATO SPEARS, PAGE 112

Appetizers + Sides

WE'VE ALL HEARD THAT HAVING THREE SUBSTANTIAL MEALS A DAY IS THE WAY to go. But what is a snack-loving girl like myself supposed to do?

The following recipes are perfect for the in-between hours, when you want something to nibble on without spoiling lunch or dinner. You'll also find recipes to entertain guests before the main event.

Peruse, find your favorites, and use them often. The Orange Moroccan Spiced Nuts (page 62) and Balasamic + Pomegranate Roasted Sweet Potato Spears (page 112) are not to be missed.

Orange Moroccan Spiced Nuts

While enjoying some drinks with friends at a local wine bar, we were served something similar to these beauties, and I had to figure out how to re-create them at home. The bold spices pair perfectly with cane sugar and maple syrup. Serve this spicy-sweet dish as the perfect appetizer or after-dinner snack.

SERVES 9	PREP TIME 5 MIN.	COOK TIME 25 MIN.	TOTAL TIME 30 MIN.

2 Tbsp (25g) organic cane sugar

1 tsp ground cinnamon

½ tsp sea salt

½ tsp ground coriander

½ tsp ground ginger

¼ tsp black pepper

⅛ tsp allspice

⅛ tsp turmeric

Pinch of cayenne pepper or ground chili

2 Tbsp (30ml) grape seed oil, avocado oil, or melted coconut oil

2 Tbsp (30ml) maple syrup or agave nectar

2¼ cups (~225g) raw nuts (pecans, walnuts, and cashews are best)

1 orange (131g)

01 Preheat the oven to 325 degrees F (162 degrees C).

02 Mix the sugar, cinnamon, salt, coriander, ginger, black pepper, allspice, turmeric, and cayenne in a small bowl and set aside.

03 Add the grape seed oil and maple syrup to a large bowl and whisk to combine. Toast the pecans on a rimmed baking sheet for 7 minutes, then add to bowl with oil/maple syrup. Toss to coat generously.

04 Add the spice mixture and toss to coat. Return the nuts to the oven and bake for 15-20 minutes more, stirring every 10 minutes or so to ensure even cooking.

05 In the meantime, peel the orange rind into small curls using a vegetable peeler or paring knife.

06 When the nuts are finished roasting, remove them from the oven and add the orange peel to the pan. Toss to coat while still warm to infuse the flavor. Taste and adjust the seasonings as desired.

07 Let cool completely, then remove the orange peel from the pan and serve. The nuts will keep covered up to 2 weeks at room temperature, though are best when fresh.

Pizza-Stuffed Mushrooms

This is the only appetizer you need for Italian night. Serve these stuffed mushrooms alongside pasta or pizza or as a stand-alone snack. The vegan cream cheese lends a smooth, creamy texture that complements the spices perfectly.

SERVES 6

PREP TIME 10 MIN. | **COOK TIME 25 MIN.** | **TOTAL TIME 35 MIN.**

16 ounces (453g) crimini or button mushrooms

1 Tbsp (15ml) grape seed oil or avocado oil

8 ounces (227g) vegan cream cheese

¼ cup (27g) red onion, finely diced

½ cup (70g) green or red bell pepper, finely diced

2 Tbsp (15g) black olives, diced (optional)

Pinch of sea salt and red pepper flakes

2 tsp Italian seasonings (or 1 tsp each dried oregano and basil)

¼ cup (20g) Vegan Parmesan (page 7), plus more for topping

PIZZA SAUCE *(for dipping)*
1 cup (245g) tomato sauce

2 tsp Italian seasonings (or 1 tsp each dried oregano and basil)

Pinch of sea salt and red pepper flakes

OPTIONAL
1-2 tsp maple syrup, organic cane sugar, or coconut sugar

01 Preheat the oven to 375 degrees F (190 degrees C). Lightly grease a rimmed baking sheet.

02 Brush the dirt from the mushrooms using a damp towel and remove stems. (Do not immerse the mushrooms in water or they will get spongy.) Lightly brush or spray the mushrooms with the grape seed oil. Set aside.

03 Mix the vegan cream cheese, onion, bell pepper, olives, salt, red pepper flakes, and Italian seasonings together in a medium bowl. Scoop generous portions into the mushrooms. Top with an extra sprinkle of Vegan Parmesan.

04 Bake the mushrooms on the prepared baking sheet for 25-27 minutes, or until the mushrooms are tender and slightly browned.

05 While the mushrooms are baking, prepare the pizza sauce. Add the tomato sauce, Italian seasonings, salt, red pepper flakes, and maple syrup, if using, to a small saucepan over medium heat. Bring to a low boil, then reduce the heat to low. Taste and adjust the seasonings as needed. Keep over a low heat until ready to serve.

06 Serve the mushrooms with additional Vegan Parmesan, red pepper flakes, and pizza sauce.

Endive Hummus Boats

Need a last-minute, easy appetizer to impress dinner guests? Try these elegant endive boats filled with your favorite hummus. My Roasted Red Pepper + Harissa Hummus (page 77) works wonderfully here, and I have found the pine nuts add the perfect finishing touch. If endive is hard to come by, simply substitute your favorite cracker or sliced cucumbers.

SERVES 6 | **PREP TIME 15 MIN.** | **TOTAL TIME 15 MIN.**

3 heads (~225g) endive lettuce, cleaned and gently pulled apart

1 cup (246g) Roasted Red Pepper and Harissa Hummus (page 77) or Simple Sun-Dried Tomato Hummus (page 82)

1 tsp chili powder

¼ cup (34g) roasted pine nuts

OPTIONAL
Fresh chopped parsley

01 Arrange the endive pieces on a serving platter or plate.

02 Scoop the hummus into a plastic sandwich or freezer bag. Snip off the very edge of one corner and gently squeeze 1-2-Tbsp into each endive leaf, or as much as will fit comfortably. Repeat until all are filled. There may be leftover hummus, which can be served with crackers, pita, or vegetables.

03 Garnish each with a pinch of chili powder, a few pine nuts, and fresh parsley (optional).

04 Chill and cover until ready to serve, up to 1 day in advance. Best when fresh.

Simple Greek Bruschetta

This 15-minute, Greek-inspired bruschetta will be an instant favorite. Fresh tomato, Kalamata olives, and herbs are married with a simple dressing of olive oil and balsamic vinegar. Pile on top of thick slices of baguette for the perfect appetizer or side dish.

SERVES 6

PREP TIME 10 MIN. | **COOK TIME 5 MIN.** | **TOTAL TIME 15 MIN.**

BREAD
1 white or wheat baguette, sliced into ¾-inch slices

1 Tbsp (15ml) olive oil, grape seed oil, or avocado oil

1 large clove garlic, halved

BRUSCHETTA
2 cups (300g) cherry tomatoes, quartered

¼ cup (40g) Kalamata olives, pitted and chopped (optional)

¼ cup (15g) fresh basil, chopped

1 Tbsp (3g) dried oregano, or 2 Tbsp fresh oregano, chopped

1 Tbsp (15ml) balsamic vinegar

1 Tbsp (15ml) olive oil

Pinch each of sea salt and black pepper

01 Preheat the oven to 425 degrees F (218 degrees C).

02 Arrange the baguette slices on a rimmed baking sheet and brush with olive oil. Take the garlic clove and rub on both sides of the slices for extra flavor. Arrange in a single layer on the baking sheet.

03 Bake the baguette slices until just slightly golden brown, about 5 minutes. Remove and set aside.

04 In the meantime, add cherry tomatoes, olives (optional), basil, oregano, vinegar, olive oil, salt, and pepper to a medium bowl. Toss to coat. Taste and adjust the seasonings as needed, adding more salt, basil, or vinegar as desired.

05 Serve with the toasted baguette slices. Store leftovers separately from the bread, covered in the refrigerator, for up to 2 days, though best when fresh.

Spinach + Artichoke Dip

*30 MINUTES OR LESS

*10 INGREDIENTS OR LESS

*GF GLUTEN-FREE

The vegan restaurant of my dreams serves this dip piping hot with chips and crisp vegetables. Until I find that restaurant, I will make my own. Soaked cashews and vegan cream cheese give this dish an extra-creamy base, while nutritional yeast and vegan parmesan cheese add plenty of rich, cheesy flavor. My favorite way to enjoy this dip is with tortilla chips. However, toasted baguette and vegetables are delightful as well.

SERVES 4 TO 6 | **PREP TIME 10 MIN.** | **COOK TIME 20 MIN.** | **TOTAL TIME 30 MIN.**

3 Tbsp (45ml) olive oil or grape seed oil

5 cloves garlic (2½ Tbsp or 15g), minced

¾ cup (90g) raw cashews, soaked and drained*

8 ounces (227g) vegan cream cheese*

½ cup (120ml) unsweetened plain almond milk or DIY Almond Milk (page 6)

4-6 Tbsp (12-18g) nutritional yeast

½ tsp each sea salt and black pepper, plus more to taste

1 14-ounce (400g) can artichoke hearts, well drained and chopped

1 pound (454g) frozen chopped spinach, thawed and squeezed dry in a thin towel

¼ cup (20g) Vegan Parmesan (page 7) for topping

FOR SERVING
Vegetables

Tortilla chips

Crackers

Toasted baguette

01 Preheat the oven to 350 degrees F (176 degrees C). Heat a large oven-safe cast-iron or metal skillet over medium heat.

02 Once the skillet is hot, add 1 Tbsp (15ml) olive oil and the garlic. Sauté for 1-2 minutes or until just golden brown. Set aside to cool.

03 To the bowl of a blender, add the cashews, garlic, vegan cream cheese, remaining 2 Tbsp (30ml) olive oil, and almond milk. Purée to a cream.

04 Add 4 Tbsp (12g) nutritional yeast to start, plus the salt and pepper. Blend once more.

05 Taste and adjust the seasonings as needed. The dip should be cheesy in flavor and well salted, so consider adding the remaining 2 Tbsp (6g) nutritional yeast and another ¼-½ tsp salt. Set aside.

06 Add the artichokes and spinach to the skillet used earlier. Pour all of the cheesy sauce over the artichokes and spinach. The mixture will look sauce-heavy, but that's the idea. Stir to combine.

07 Sprinkle the top with Vegan Parmesan for additional texture/flavor. Bake for 8-12 minutes, or until warmed through.

continued

08 Serve warm with assorted vegetables, tortilla chips, crackers, or toasted baguette, tortilla chips being my personal favorite.

09 Store leftovers covered in the refrigerator for 3-4 days, though best when fresh. Reheat in an oven-safe dish at 350 degree F until warmed through (or in the microwave), adding more almond milk if the dip dries out.

Notes

*Soak the cashews for 6-8 hours in cool water, or pour boiling water over them and let rest uncovered at room temperature for 1 hour. Drain well and use as instructed.

*If you don't have vegan cream cheese, omit and add another ⅔ cup (90g) cashews (soaked). However, the dip will not be as creamy.

Best Ever 20-Minute Vegan Queso

Dare I say this is my favorite vegan queso yet? This is easily the creamiest, most flavorful queso sauce, perfect for your next nacho bar. Enjoy with tortilla chips, or on nachos, burritos, or tacos! Take Mexican dishes to the next level with this simple, undetectably vegan queso.

SERVES 6

PREP TIME 5 MIN. | COOK TIME 15 MIN. | TOTAL TIME 20 MIN.

3 Tbsp (42g) vegan butter (or substitute grape seed oil or avocado oil)

4 cloves garlic, minced (2 Tbsp or 12g)

¼ cup (34g) unbleached all-purpose flour*

1¾-2 cups (420-480ml) unsweetened plain almond milk, DIY Almond Milk (page 6), or rice milk

½ cup (24g) nutritional yeast

½ tsp sea salt

¼ tsp ground cumin

¼ tsp chili powder

1 Tbsp (15ml) maple syrup (or substitute organic cane sugar)

OPTIONAL
¼ tsp hot sauce

4 Tbsp (64g) chunky salsa (or canned diced tomatoes with peppers or chilies)

01 Heat a large skillet or saucepan over medium heat. Once hot, add the butter and let it melt and start to sizzle, about 1 minute.

02 Add the garlic and stir to disperse. Cook for 1-2 minutes, stirring frequently, then reduce the heat if the garlic starts to brown too quickly.

03 Add the flour 1 Tbsp (8½g) at a time and whisk (see the note for the gluten-free version). Cook for 1 minute, then whisk in the almond milk ½ cup (120ml) at a time until it no longer looks thick and lumpy, about 1¾ cups total.

04 Cook in the skillet for 2 minutes, then transfer to the bowl of a high-speed blender. Add the nutritional yeast, salt, cumin, chili powder, maple syrup, and hot sauce (optional). Blend on high until creamy and smooth.

05 Taste and adjust the seasonings as needed, adding more nutritional yeast for extra cheesiness, salt for savoriness, sweetener for flavor balance, or dry spices for depth of flavor.

06 Transfer back to the skillet and simmer on low for 5 minutes, stirring often, to thicken.

continued

07 Turn off heat and use a slotted spoon to add chunky salsa or diced tomatoes and chilies (optional). Stir to combine.

08 Serve hot with chips, on burrito bowls (see page 141), nachos (see page 156), or enchiladas (see page 161).

09 Best when fresh, but will keep in the refrigerator for up to 3-4 days. Reheat in a microwave or small saucepan until hot and bubbly.

Note

*To keep this queso gluten-free, simply substitute cornstarch or arrowroot starch for flour and proceed through the recipe as instructed. It will look more clumpy initially, but when blended it works the same.

Roasted Red Pepper + Harissa Hummus

This creamy blend of red bell pepper and harissa paste is the perfect combination of spicy and sweet in a hummus. Enjoy it with vegetables and pita, or upgrade your next lunch by using it as a spread for veggie sandwiches.

SERVES 12

PREP TIME 15 MIN. | **COOK TIME 35 MIN.** | **TOTAL TIME 50 MIN.**

1 red bell pepper (119g)

3 cloves garlic
(1½ Tbsp or 9g)

1 15-ounce (425g) can
chickpeas, slightly
drained

¼ cup (56g) tahini

1 lemon, juiced
(2 Tbsp or 30ml)

½ tsp sea salt, or to taste

¼ tsp smoked paprika

1-2 tsp harissa paste*

3-4 Tbsp (45-60ml)
olive oil, plus more for
drizzling

OPTIONAL
Paprika, chili powder,
and/or chili garlic
sauce, and parsley for
garnish

Note

*If you do not have harissa
paste, omit or substitute
1 heaping Tbsp (~20g)
tomato paste and ¼ tsp
each coriander, cumin, and
caraway, 1 tsp ground chili,
and one extra pinch salt.

01 Preheat the oven to 400 degrees F (204 degrees C). Line a rimmed baking sheet with foil.

02 Once the oven is preheated, place the bell pepper on the prepared baking sheet and roast for a total of 30-35 minutes, turning every 15 minutes until charred on all sides.

03 Either leave the garlic raw for more spice or roast (see page 9) for a sweeter flavor.

04 Remove the bell pepper from the oven and wrap in foil. Let rest for 3-4 minutes. Then peel off the skin and remove the seeds and stem. Set aside.

05 Add all of the ingredients to the bowl of a food processor or blender. Blend until creamy and smooth.

06 Serve immediately, or refrigerate for up to 2-3 hours to firm. To serve, drizzle with olive oil and a sprinkle of paprika, chili powder, and fresh parsley (optional).

07 Leftovers keep fresh covered in the refrigerator for 7-10 days.

Southwest Sweet Potato Black Bean Dip

I am a sucker for a good dip, especially when chips are involved. Infused with Southwest flavors and loaded with good-for-you whole foods, this dish can be enjoyed guilt-free. Serve as an appetizer or side dish on Mexican night. It's also great as a topping for burrito bowls, tacos, nachos, and more!

SERVES 6

PREP TIME 10 MIN. | COOK TIME 20 MIN. | TOTAL TIME 30 MIN.

2 medium to large organic sweet potatoes (~260g), cubed, skin on

2 Tbsp (30ml) olive oil or avocado oil

2 Tbsp (30ml) maple syrup (or substitute coconut sugar)

¼ tsp each sea salt, chili powder, ground cinnamon, and ground cumin

1 cup (150g) whole corn kernels

1 cup (60g) cilantro, chopped

½ cup red onion (55g), diced

1 15-ounce (425g) can black beans, rinsed and drained

SAUCE
1 ripe avocado

1 Tbsp (15ml) olive oil or avocado oil

1 lime, juiced (3 Tbsp or 45ml)

1-2 Tbsp (15-30ml) maple syrup or agave nectar

Pinch each of sea salt and black pepper

01 Preheat the oven to 375 degrees F (190 degrees C).

02 Lightly grease a rimmed baking sheet and add the sweet potatoes, olive oil, maple syrup, salt, chili powder, cinnamon, and cumin. Toss to coat.

03 Bake for 20 minutes or until soft and lightly browned, stirring once halfway through to ensure even baking. Sample and adjust the seasonings if needed. Set aside.

04 In the meantime, prepare the sauce: Add the avocado, olive oil, lime juice, maple syrup, salt, and pepper to a large bowl. Mash/mix to combine. Taste and adjust the seasonings as desired.

05 Add the corn, cilantro, onion, black beans, and roasted sweet potatoes to the sauce and toss to combine. Taste and adjust the seasonings if needed.

06 Serve at room temperature with tortilla chips. Store leftovers covered in the refrigerator for 2-3 days, though best when fresh.

Creamy Tomato + Herb Bisque

This creamy tomato bisque is my take on the classic. To keep my version dairy-free, I rely on coconut milk for rich, creamy texture; dill, garlic, and basil for depth of flavor; and red pepper flakes for a touch of heat. This is the perfect, hearty soup to enjoy on a cold day and is excellent with a veggie sandwich or salad. Don't forget the garlic croutons!

SERVES 4

PREP TIME 5 MIN. | **COOK TIME 25 MIN.** | **TOTAL TIME 30 MIN.**

1 28-ounce (793g) can crushed or peeled tomatoes, in juices

1 6-ounce (170g) can tomato paste

1 cup (240ml) water (substitute up to half with extra coconut milk for creamier soup)

1 14-ounce (414ml) can light coconut milk

1 Tbsp (3g) dried dill [or 2 Tbsp (5g) fresh dill, minced]

1 Tbsp (8g) garlic powder

1 tsp dried basil or 2 tsp fresh basil, minced, plus more for serving

½ tsp each sea salt and black pepper

Pinch of red pepper flakes (optional)

3 Tbsp (45ml) maple syrup or substitute coconut sugar

GARLIC CROUTONS
2 cups (70g) rustic white or wheat bread, cut into 1-inch cubes

01 Add all of the soup ingredients to large saucepan or pot and bring to a simmer.

02 Transfer to the bowl of a blender, or use an immersion blender, to purée the soup. Then transfer the soup back to the saucepan and bring to a simmer over medium-low heat. Taste and adjust the seasonings as needed.

03 Let simmer on low uncovered for at least 10-15 minutes more. The longer it simmers, the deeper the flavor develops.

04 As the soup simmers, prepare the croutons. Preheat the oven to 325 degrees F (162 degrees C). Add the bread cubes to a large bowl.

05 In a separate bowl, whisk together the grape seed oil, garlic powder, salt, pepper, oregano, and basil. Pour over bread cubes and toss to combine. Season with a bit more garlic powder, salt, and pepper. Toss once more.

06 Spread the bread cubes onto a rimmed baking sheet and bake for 15-20 minutes, or until golden brown. Stir/toss at the 10-minute mark to ensure even baking.

3 Tbsp (45ml) grape seed
oil or avocado oil

¼ tsp each garlic powder,
sea salt, black pepper,
dried oregano, and dried
basil

07 Taste the soup and adjust the
seasonings as needed. Then serve with the
croutons, more fresh dill or basil, and a
touch of pepper.

08 Leftovers keep covered in the
refrigerator for 4-5 days or in the
freezer for up to 1 month.

Simple Sun-Dried Tomato Hummus

If you love the rich flavor of tomatoes, you will love this simple sun-dried tomato hummus. It is infused with oregano and fresh lemon for flavor and a kick of brightness. You will want to bring this to parties, picnics, road trips, and everywhere in between. It's so delicious and creamy, especially on a good cracker.

SERVES 10

PREP TIME 15 MIN. | **TOTAL TIME 15 MIN.**

1 15-ounce (425g) can chickpeas, slightly drained some liquid reserved (to add to hummus)

4 cloves garlic (2 Tbsp or 12g), minced

½ cup (60g) loosely packed sun-dried tomatoes (if in oil, drain)

¼ cup (56g) tahini

2 lemons, juiced (4 Tbsp or 60ml)

¾ tsp sea salt

1 tsp dried oregano

¼ cup (60ml) olive oil, plus more for serving

Water to thin

GARNISHES *(optional)*
Toasted pine nuts

Smoked paprika

01 Add all of the ingredients to the bowl of a blender or food processor. Blend until creamy and smooth, scraping down the sides as needed. Add water if there is trouble blending (I added ½ cup or 120ml). Taste and adjust the seasonings as desired.

02 Garnish with additional olive oil, paprika, and toasted pine nuts (optional). Serve with pita, crackers, or vegetables.

03 Leftovers will keep covered in the refrigerator for at least 7-10 days.

"Cheddar" Beer Soup

Beer fan or not, you will love this creamy, 1-pot soup. Blonde ale imparts a slight bitterness that complements the nutritional yeast's cheese flavor well. This is a wonderful soup to enjoy during the fall and winter months when you're craving something hearty and warming. Top with garlic croutons or sautéed vegetables for extra heartiness.

SERVES 4

| PREP TIME 10 MIN. | COOK TIME 45 MIN. | TOTAL TIME 55 MIN. |

3 Tbsp (45ml) olive oil (or substitute vegan butter)

5 cloves garlic, minced (2½ Tbsp or 15g)

½ white or yellow onion (55g), diced

1 pound (453g) Yukon gold potatoes, cut into bite-size pieces, skin on

Sea salt and black pepper, to taste

3 Tbsp (25g) all-purpose flour*

1 cup (240ml) golden ale, plus more for a stronger beer flavor*

1 cup (240ml) plain unsweetened almond milk or DIY Almond Milk (page 6)

2 cups (480ml) vegetable broth

¼ cup plus 1 Tbsp (15g) nutritional yeast, plus more to taste

1 Tbsp (15ml) maple syrup (or substitute organic cane sugar or coconut sugar)

01 Heat a large pot or saucepan over medium heat. Once hot, add the olive oil, garlic, and onion. Stir and cook for 1-2 minutes. Then add the potatoes.

02 Season with a healthy pinch of salt and pepper, then cover and cook for 4 minutes.

03 Add the flour and stir to coat the potatoes. Cook for 1 minute. Then add the beer. Stir and cook for 3-4 minutes, or until reduced by about half. The sauce should be fairly thick.

04 Add the almond milk, broth, nutritional yeast, maple syrup, and another pinch of salt and pepper. Bring to a simmer and reduce the heat to low. Simmer for 20-30 minutes, or until potatoes are fork tender.

05 Transfer three-fourths of the soup to the bowl of a blender (or use an immersion blender to gently blend majority of soup). Purée until creamy and smooth, scraping down the sides as needed.

06 Taste and adjust the seasonings if needed, adding more salt, pepper, and nutritional yeast as desired.

07 If the soup appears too thin, add 1 Tbsp (8½g) flour (or cornstarch or arrowroot starch) and blend for added thickness. It will thicken when returned to heat.

continued

08 Return the soup to pot and bring back to a simmer. Then cover and let cook for at least another 5-10 minutes, or until the potatoes have taken on the flavor of the soup.

09 Serve hot. For garnish, try garlic croutons (see Creamy Tomato + Herb Bisque on page 80 for recipe), fresh parsley, or thinly sliced, lightly sautéed Brussels sprouts (pictured above).

10 Store leftovers in the refrigerator for 3-5 days, or in the freezer up to 1 month.

Note

*To keep this soup gluten-free, substitute cornstarch or arrowroot starch for the all-purpose flour and proceed as instructed. Be sure to blend the soup, as I find starches tend to lump. Also, make sure to use a gluten-free beer.

Creamy Broccoli + "Cheddar" Soup

It's been a long time since I enjoyed a classic broccoli and cheese soup. This dairy-free version satisfies my craving with an ultra-creamy, cheesy, and hearty base. The butternut squash has a vibrant orange hue that complements the bright green broccoli perfectly. Top with garlic croutons for extra heartiness.

SERVES 4

PREP TIME 5 MIN. | **COOK TIME 25 MIN.** | **TOTAL TIME 30 MIN.**

2 Tbsp (30ml) olive oil, grape seed oil, or coconut oil

3 cloves garlic, minced (1½ Tbsp or 9g)

3 cups (420g) cubed butternut squash

Pinch of sea salt and black pepper, plus more to taste

2 cups (480ml) unsweetened plain almond milk or DIY Almond Milk (page 6)

2 cups (480ml) vegetable broth

½ cup (24g) nutritional yeast, plus more to taste

3 cups (273g) broccoli, loosely chopped

⅛ tsp ground nutmeg

½ tsp garlic powder

½ tsp apple cider vinegar or lemon juice, for brightness

1-2 Tbsp (15-30ml) maple syrup or coconut sugar

continued

01 Heat a large pot over medium heat. Once hot, add the olive oil, garlic, and butternut squash. Season with a healthy pinch of salt and pepper.

02 Cover and cook for 4 minutes, stirring occasionally, or until the squash is soft and golden brown. If it's browning too quickly, slightly reduce the heat.

03 Add the almond milk, broth, and nutritional yeast. Season once more with a pinch of salt and pepper. Bring to a low boil.

04 Add the broccoli, nutmeg, garlic powder, vinegar, maple syrup, and red pepper flakes (optional). Stir to combine. Cover and let simmer 5-6 minutes.

05 Scoop out about 1 cup broccoli using a slotted spoon. Set aside for a later use.

06 Transfer the soup to the bowl of a blender. (Or use an immersion blender to blend the soup in the pot.) Add the cornstarch for thickening (optional). Purée until creamy and smooth.

07 Taste and adjust the seasonings as needed, adding more salt, pepper, nutritional yeast, or nutmeg to taste. I add more of each as I prefer a very cheesy, savory soup.

continued

OPTIONAL

⅛ tsp red pepper flakes

2 Tbsp (16g) cornstarch or arrowroot starch, for thickening

08 Return the soup to the pot. Bring to a simmer over medium-low heat to thicken, stirring occasionally. Once simmering, add the broccoli reserved from earlier and heat for a few minutes.

09 For a thicker soup, add more cornstarch 1 tablespoon at a time, whisking into a separate portion of the soup and then adding it back to the pot to avoid clumps, until the desired consistency is reached. This, however, is optional.

10 This soup is excellent served with your favorite rustic bread, a veggie sandwich (see page 168), or garlic croutons (find the method in my Creamy Tomato + Herb Bisque recipe, page 80).

11 Leftovers keep covered in the refrigerator for 5-6 days or in the freezer for 1 month.

The House Salad

Every household needs a house salad—this is mine. Crispy, fresh vegetables are topped with a vibrant hummus–based dressing. I love this recipe for its texture and flavor, but mostly because I always have the ingredients on hand, so it's easy to make. This is the perfect, refreshing salad to accompany any entrée.

SERVES 1

PREP TIME 10 MIN. | **TOTAL TIME 10 MIN.**

DRESSING

2 Tbsp (30g) plain hummus

½ lemon, juiced

¼ tsp dried dill

¼ tsp garlic powder

1-2 tsp maple syrup

SALAD

2 cups (94g) chopped romaine lettuce

4 cherry tomatoes (68g)

¼ cup carrots (32g), diced

¼ cup red onion (27g), diced

¼ ripe avocado, cubed

1 tsp hemp seeds

01 Whisk together the hummus, lemon juice, dill, garlic powder, and maple syrup in a small bowl. Taste and adjust the seasonings as needed. Thin with water (if desired) until pourable.

02 Add all of the salad ingredients to a small serving bowl. Add the dressing and toss to coat.

03 Leftovers keep well (separated) covered in the refrigerator for 2-3 days. Multiply ingredients by the number of people for a larger salad.

Balsamic Tomato + Tofu Salad

This is my vegan homage to the classic caprese salad. It has thick slices of ripe tomatoes stacked with fresh basil and my Herb-Marinated Tofu. It is then drizzled with balsamic vinegar. This makes the perfect appetizer or side dish to any Italian entrée.

SERVES 4 | **PREP TIME 5 MIN.** | **TOTAL TIME 5 MIN.**

2 ripe tomatoes (246g), cut into ¼-inch slices

1 cup (124g) Herb-Marinated Tofu (page 203)

1 cup (~60g) basil leaves

¼ cup (60ml) balsamic vinegar

01 Layer the tomato slices with 3-4 cubes marinated tofu and 1-2 basil leaves per layer.

02 Continue stacking to the desired height, then drizzle with balsamic vinegar (or balsamic reduction*) and serve. Best when fresh.

Note

*For a more intense balsamic flavor, reduce 1 cup (240ml) balsamic vinegar in a small saucepan over medium heat for 20-30 minutes. Reduce the heat to low when it begins boiling, and simmer until it's thickened and reduced by about half. You'll know it's done when you run a spatula across the bottom of the pan and it leaves a line. Let cool before using.

Coconut Red Curry Vegetable Soup

On a trip to Mexico, John and I landed exhausted and hungry and a red curry soup was the first thing we dipped into. It was comforting and just what we were craving. My 1-pot version is rich, creamy, and subtly sweet thanks to coconut milk, and gets loads of flavor from red curry paste, garlic, and ginger. It's the perfect soup to warm up to on cold days, and is especially delicious alongside spring rolls and curry dishes.

SERVES 4	PREP TIME 5 MIN.	COOK TIME 20 MIN.	TOTAL TIME 25 MIN.

1 Tbsp (15ml) coconut oil

¼ cup (32g) diced carrots

1 cup (80g) diced green onion

¼ tsp each sea salt and black pepper, plus more to taste

1 large clove garlic, minced (~1 Tbsp or 6g)

2 Tbsp (30g) red curry paste (or 1-2 Tbsp [8-16g] curry powder)

1 cup (54g) white button mushrooms, wiped clean and sliced

¾ cup (112g) fresh tomato, diced

2 1-inch slices fresh ginger or 1 tsp ground ginger

2 14-ounce (414ml) cans light coconut milk*

¼ tsp ground turmeric

1-2 Tbsp (15-30ml) maple syrup (or coconut sugar)

01 Heat a large saucepan over medium heat. Once hot, add the coconut oil, carrots, and green onions. Cook for 2 minutes. Season with a healthy pinch of salt and pepper.

02 Add the garlic and curry paste. Stir. Cook 2-3 minutes, stirring frequently.

03 Add the mushrooms, tomatoes, and ginger. Stir once more. Season with another pinch of salt.

04 Cook for 3 minutes. (If substituting any vegetable broth for coconut milk, hold back on the salt as the broth will add plenty of flavor.)

05 Add the coconut milk, turmeric, and maple syrup. Whisk. Bring to a very low boil over medium heat, then reduce the heat to low.

06 Simmer for 10-15 minutes, or until the carrots are cooked through and the curry flavor has permeated the vegetables.

07 Taste and adjust the seasonings as needed, adding more maple syrup for sweetness, or salt.

08 Discard the ginger and serve warm as a soup, or serve over cooked jasmine rice or Cauliflower Rice (page 8).

09 Garnish with cilantro and fresh lime juice (optional) for extra flavor. Best when fresh.

OPTIONAL
Fresh cilantro, chopped

Fresh lime juice

Notes

*Substitute the second can coconut milk with 1½ cups (360ml) vegetable broth for a lighter soup. Reduce the salt, as the broth will be naturally saltier.

*Add rice noodles for extra texture. Add in when the coconut milk is boiling. Cover and cook until soft, about 10 minutes, stirring frequently.

Greek Kale Salad

This is a classic Greek salad upgraded with kale, chickpeas, and a lemony, garlic-herb dressing. This salad is hearty enough to be a stand-alone entrée, but it also makes a fantastic side dish to Mediterranean dishes.

SERVES 2 AS ENTRÉE, 4 AS SIDE | **PREP TIME 20 MIN.** | **COOK TIME 10 MIN.** | **TOTAL TIME 30 MIN.**

1 red bell pepper (119g), thinly sliced

2 Tbsp (30ml) olive oil

1 large bundle of kale (~4 cups or 268g), loosely chopped

1 Tbsp (15ml) lemon juice

¼ red onion (27g), thinly sliced

½ cup (75g) cherry tomatoes, halved

¼ cup (40g) Kalamata olives, pitted and halved

½ cup (82g) cooked chickpeas

½ cucumber, thinly sliced (optional)

GARLIC HERB DRESSING
¼ cup (60g) hummus*

½ lemon, juiced (1 Tbsp or 15ml)

¾-1 tsp dried dill or 2-3 tsp fresh dill

3 cloves garlic, minced (1½ Tbsp or 9g)

1-2 Tbsp (15-30ml) water, or unsweetened almond milk, or DIY Almond Milk (page 6) to thin

01 In a skillet over medium heat, sauté the bell pepper in 1 Tbsp (15ml) olive oil until slightly browned and soft, about 5 minutes. (Or leave raw, if desired.) Set aside.

02 To prepare the dressing, add the hummus, the lemon juice, dill, and garlic to a small bowl. Whisk to combine. Add only enough water to thin until the dressing is pourable. Taste and adjust the seasonings as needed.

03 Add the kale to large bowl and add lemon juice and remaining 1 Tbsp (15ml) olive oil. Use your hands to massage the kale to break down its texture and remove some of the bitterness.

04 Add the roasted bell pepper, onion, cherry tomatoes, olives, chickpeas, and cucumber (optional).

05 Add the desired amount of dressing and toss to coat. Serve immediately. Store leftovers separately in the refrigerator for 2-3 days. Best when fresh.

Note

*If you do not have hummus, tahini makes a great substitute for the dressing. Adjust seasonings—adding more salt, lemon juice, garlic, and dill—to compensate.

Beet, Orange + Walnut Salad with Lemon Tahini Dressing

If you are in need of a new way to enjoy beets, look no further. Simple and colorful, this elegant salad is perfect for entertaining and utilizes some of winter's most gorgeous produce. The recipe generously serves two, boasting 16 grams of protein per serving!

SERVES 2 | **PREP TIME 5 MIN.** | **COOK TIME 25 MIN.** | **TOTAL TIME 30 MIN.**

3 medium beets (~246g), peeled and cut into ¼-inch discs (halve large pieces)

1 Tbsp (15ml) grape seed oil, avocado oil, or coconut oil

Pinch each of sea salt and black pepper

½ cup (60g) raw walnuts, halved, or hazelnuts

2 large oranges (~262g), peel sliced off and cut into ¼-inch rounds (or peeled and segmented)

Fresh parsley, chopped (optional)

DRESSING
¼ cup (56g) tahini

1 lemon, juiced (2 Tbsp or 30ml)

1-2 Tbsp (15-30ml) maple syrup

2-4 Tbsp (30-60ml) hot water to thin

01 Preheat the oven to 400 degrees F (204 degrees C) and line a rimmed baking sheet with foil or parchment paper.

02 Place the beets on the prepared baking sheet. Drizzle with grape seed oil and a pinch each of salt and pepper. Toss to combine, then arrange on two-thirds of the baking sheet (making room for the walnuts later on). Roast for 15 minutes, then remove the pan from the oven and add the walnuts to the empty side of the pan.

03 Bake for another 8-10 minutes, or until the nuts are fragrant and golden brown. Remove the pan from the oven to cool slightly.

04 In the meantime, prepare the dressing by whisking together the tahini, lemon juice, and maple syrup. Add hot water until the desired consistency is reached. Taste and adjust the seasonings as needed.

05 Plate the beets and orange segments in a circular arrangement (optional). Top with the toasted walnuts. Serve with the dressing.

06 For extra color, garnish with fresh parsley (optional). Alternatively, serve on a bed of baby spinach or mixed greens. Best when fresh.

Garlic "Cheddar" Herb Biscuits

If you've ever longed for the cheesy, garlicky, herbaceous goodness that is the Red Lobster biscuit, this recipe is for you. Loaded with fresh garlic, herbs, and nutritional yeast, this will convince anyone that they're eating the real thing. These are a perfect appetizer or accompaniment alongside almost any entrée, but I prefer mine next to creamy pastas and soups.

SERVES 8

PREP TIME 10 MIN. | **COOK TIME 12 MIN.** | **TOTAL TIME 22 MIN.**

1 scant cup (~230ml) unsweetened plain almond milk or DIY Almond Milk (page 6)

1 Tbsp (15ml) freshly squeezed lemon juice or vinegar

2 cups (238-272g) unbleached all-purpose flour

3½ Tbsp (10g) nutritional yeast, plus more to taste

1 Tbsp (13g) baking powder

½ tsp baking soda

¾ tsp sea salt

½ tsp garlic powder

4 Tbsp (56g) cold vegan butter, plus more for topping*

2 cloves garlic, minced (1 Tbsp or 6g)

2-3 Tbsp (69g) chives, finely diced

01 Preheat the oven to 450 degrees F (232 degrees C).

02 Measure out the almond milk in a liquid measuring cup and add the lemon juice. Let rest for 5 minutes.

03 In the meantime, add the flour, nutritional yeast, baking powder, baking soda, salt, and garlic powder to a large bowl and whisk to combine.

04 Add the butter, garlic, and chives and use a pastry cutter or fork to combine until only small pieces remain and the mixture looks like wet sand. Work quickly so the butter does not get too warm.

05 Make a well in the dry ingredients. Use a wooden spoon to stir gently while pouring in the almond milk mixture ¼ cup (60ml) at a time. Add only as much almond milk as is needed to form a sticky dough. (Not all of the almond milk mixture may be needed.)

06 Turn the dough onto a lightly floured surface, dusting the top of the dough with a bit of flour. Very gently turn over on itself 5 or 6 times, barely kneading.

07 Form into a 1-inch-thick disc, handling the dough as little as possible. Then use

continued

a 1-inch-thick biscuit cutter or similar-shaped object with sharp edges
(such as a cookie cutter or cocktail shaker) to push straight down
through the dough. Slightly twist.

08 Repeat and place the biscuits on a baking sheet in two rows, making
sure they just touch—this will help them rise uniformly.

09 Gently re-form the dough scraps. Cut out 1 or 2 more biscuits and
repeat until all of the dough is used—there should be 8-10 biscuits,
depending on the size of your cutter.

10 Brush the tops of the biscuits with a bit more melted butter and
gently press a small divot in the center using two fingers. This will
help them rise evenly and prevent the middle from forming a dome.

11 Bake for 12-15 minutes, or until fluffy and light golden brown.
Serve immediately with another brush of melted butter (optional).

12 Let the remaining biscuits cool completely before storing in an
airtight container or bag. Will keep for 2-3 days at room temperature.

13 These biscuits can be served with breakfast or dinner and are
excellent alongside my Creamy Tomato and Herb Bisque (see page 80).

Note

*Substitute chilled (scoopable) refined coconut
oil for vegan butter with varied results.

Garlic Scalloped Potatoes

Hello, Thanksgiving! I created this recipe with the holidays in mind. It will easily stand up to your aunt Betty's scalloped potatoes that are loaded with butter, cheese, and cornflakes. The difference is this dish is dairy-free, yet remains insanely delicious. No need to save this one for the holidays—enjoy it year-round.

SERVES 4

PREP TIME 15 MIN.	COOK TIME 1 HR. 5 MIN.	TOTAL TIME 1 HR. 20 MIN.

2 ½ Tbsp (38ml) olive oil or grape seed oil

4 cloves garlic (2 Tbsp or 12g), minced

¼ tsp each sea salt and black pepper, plus more to taste

2½ Tbsp (21g) unbleached all-purpose flour*

1½ cups (360ml) unsweetened plain almond milk or DIY Almond Milk (page 6)

½ cup (120ml) vegetable broth

4-5 Tbsp (12-15g) nutritional yeast

⅛ tsp ground nutmeg

2-3 Yukon gold potatoes (440-660g), very thinly sliced

¼ cup (20g) Vegan Parmesan (page 7)

OPTIONAL
¼ tsp paprika

01 Preheat the oven to 350 degrees F (176 degrees C). Heat a 12-inch cast-iron skillet (or metal skillet with tall edges) over medium heat.

02 Once the skillet is hot, add the olive oil, garlic, salt, and pepper. Sauté for 1-2 minutes, stirring frequently, until just lightly golden brown.

03 Add the flour 1 Tbsp (8g) at a time, whisking to incorporate between additions. Cook for 1 minute.

04 Add the almond milk a little at a time, whisking to incorporate. Be sure not to flood the pan. Whisk and go slowly to prevent clumps from forming. Continue until all of the almond milk has been added, then add the broth. Whisk to combine.

05 Reduce the heat to low and let simmer for 4-5 minutes to thicken, whisking frequently.

06 Turn heat the off and remove the skillet from the burner. Carefully transfer the sauce to the bowl of a blender and add the nutmeg and a pinch more of salt, pepper, and nutritional yeast.

continued

07 Blend on high until creamy and smooth. Taste and adjust the seasonings as needed, adding more nutmeg, salt, pepper, or nutritional yeast to taste. The mixture should be very cheesy and savory to season the potatoes well, so don't be timid.

08 Rinse out the skillet (or grab an 8 × 8-inch baking dish) and generously grease with oil or vegan butter all the way up the sides. Add half of the sliced potatoes and season with salt and pepper. Toss to coat, then lay flat and sprinkle on 2 Tbsp (10g) Vegan Parmesan.

09 Add the remaining potatoes (only as many as will fit comfortably in the pan). Season with a bit more salt and pepper and loosely toss.

10 Add the remaining 2 Tbsp (10g) Vegan Parmesan and pour the sauce over the potatoes. The sauce should just cover the potatoes, so remove any potatoes that are above the surface. Sprinkle the top with paprika (optional).

11 Cover with foil and bake on the middle rack of the oven for 20 minutes, then remove the foil and bake for another 40-45 minutes (a total of 1 hour to 1 hour 5 minutes).

12 The potatoes are done when a knife inserted into the potatoes comes out without effort, and the top is golden brown and bubbly.

13 Remove from the oven and let cool for 10 minutes before serving. As an optional garnish, top with fresh parsley and a dash more of paprika for extra color.

Note
*Keep this recipe gluten-free by substituting cornstarch or arrowroot starch in place of the all-purpose flour.

Raspberry Spinach Ribbon Salad

This recipe is a nod to a spinach salad I used to order at a local Italian restaurant when I was growing up. I remember craving it so badly I would walk in by myself and eat it at a table for one. Ribboning the spinach provides a fancy touch, the almonds add a delicious crunch, and the raspberry vinaigrette marries everything together beautifully.

SERVES 4	PREP TIME 10 MIN.	COOK TIME 20 MIN.	TOTAL TIME 30 MIN.

DRESSING
¾ cup (180ml) balsamic vinegar

⅓ cup (80ml) olive oil

⅔ cup (80g) fresh raspberries

Pinch each of sea salt and black pepper

1-2 Tbsp (15-30ml) maple syrup, or to taste

ONIONS
½ cup (120ml) red wine vinegar

½ cup (120ml) water

1 Tbsp (12g) organic cane sugar

¼ tsp sea salt

½ red onion (55g), thinly sliced

SALAD
1 cup (112g) slivered raw almonds

4 cups (268g) raw spinach or kale, thinly sliced into "ribbons"

1½ cups (180g) fresh raspberries or strawberries

OPTIONAL
1 Tbsp (12g) chia seeds

01 Preheat the oven to 325 degrees F (162 degrees C).

02 Prepare the dressing: Heat a small saucepan over medium heat. Add the balsamic vinegar. When it reaches a low boil, reduce the heat to medium-low and continue cooking for 15-20 minutes, or until reduced by half. Set aside.

03 In the meantime, prepare the onions: Combine the red wine vinegar, water, sugar, and salt in a small bowl or mason jar. Whisk or shake to combine. Add the onion, cover, and place in the refrigerator to infuse/pickle for 15 minutes.

04 Prepare the salad: Place the slivered almonds on a rimmed baking sheet and bake for 7-10 minutes, or until slightly golden brown. Set aside.

05 Add the reduced balsamic vinegar and remaining dressing ingredients to the bowl of a food processor or blender. Blend to combine. Taste and adjust the seasonings as needed.

06 Place the spinach, raspberries, pickled onions and chia seeds (optional) in a large bowl. Top with the almonds and desired amount of dressing. Toss to coat. Serve immediately.

07 Leftovers keep (separately) in the refrigerator for 2-3 days, though best when fresh.

Parmesan Garlic Green Beans

This has been my go-to side dish for years now. It's simple, quick, and a crowd pleaser. I love how the high heat chars the outside of the beans while keeping the insides tender. A dusting of Vegan Parmesan (page 7) is the perfect finishing touch.

SERVES 4

PREP TIME 5 MIN. | **COOK TIME 12 MIN.** | **TOTAL TIME 17 MIN.**

1 pound (453g) green beans, trimmed

2 Tbsp (28g) vegan butter (or substitute grape seed oil or avocado oil)

½ tsp each sea salt and black pepper, plus more to taste.

1 tsp garlic powder, plus more to taste

3-4 Tbsp (15-20g) Vegan Parmesan (page 7), plus more for serving

01 Steam the green beans in a large bowl (covered) in the microwave for 3 minutes or on the stovetop in a vegetable steamer. Steam until slightly tender. Refrain from fully cooking.

02 Heat a large skillet over medium-high heat. Once hot, add the butter and the steamed green beans. Make sure no excess liquid gets into the pan.

03 Season with salt, pepper, and garlic powder. Toss to coat. Cover and cook for a total of 7-9 minutes, tossing frequently. Reduce the heat if browning too quickly. For slightly crispier green beans, remove the lid for the second half of cooking.

04 Once the green beans are browned and soft, add the Vegan Parmesan. Toss to coat. The skin should be well roasted with lots of flavor, so adjust the seasonings accordingly.

05 Serve with extra Vegan Parmesan. Leftovers keep covered in the refrigerator for 2-3 days, though best when fresh.

Vegan Kale Caesar Salad

Caesar salads were my favorite before I went dairy-free, and I have missed them. But this recipe has satisfied those cravings. Kale provides a hearty base, while the cashew-based dressing loaded with capers, roasted garlic, and lemon brings the whole dish to life. Hemp seeds and vegan parmesan cheese provide a finishing touch and a boost of added nutrition.

SERVES 4

PREP TIME 15 MIN. | **COOK TIME 45 MIN.** | **TOTAL TIME 60 MIN.**

DRESSING

1 cup (120g) raw cashews, quick soaked*

1 tsp Dijon mustard

1 head of Roasted Garlic (page 9)

¼ tsp each sea salt and black pepper, plus more to taste

2 cloves fresh garlic (1 Tbsp or 6g), chopped

½ cup (69g) capers [plus 2-3 Tbsp (30-45ml) brine juice from capers]

1 lemon, juiced (2 Tbsp or 30ml)

3-4 Tbsp (45-60ml) olive oil

SALAD

1 large bundle (8 ounces or 227g) of lacinato or curly kale, chopped or torn

1 Tbsp (15ml) olive oil

1 Tbsp (15ml) freshly squeezed lemon juice

¼ cup (20g) Vegan Parmesan (page 7)

2 Tbsp (20g) hemp seeds (optional)

01 Add the cashews, mustard, Roasted Garlic, salt, pepper, fresh garlic, capers and caper brine, lemon juice, and olive oil to the bowl of a blender. Blend until creamy and smooth, scraping down the sides as needed. Add enough water to thin until thick but pourable.

02 Taste and adjust the seasonings as needed, adding more lemon juice or mustard for zing, or salt or capers for saltiness. Set aside.

03 Prepare the salad: Add the kale to a large bowl. Drizzle with the olive oil and lemon juice. Use your hands to massage the kale to remove some of the bitterness and soften the texture.

04 Add desired amount of dressing, Vegan Parmesan, and hemp seeds, if using. Toss to coat and serve immediately. There will be leftover dressing, which will keep covered in the refrigerator up to 10 days.

Note

*To quick-soak the cashews, pour boiling water over the cashews. Let rest uncovered at room temperature for 1 hour. Drain well and use as instructed.

Balsamic + Pomegranate Roasted Sweet Potato Spears

I have always loved sweet potatoes, but this dish takes the obsession to a whole new level. It's simple and unexpected, and the flavors are bold and intense. Serve this as an appetizer, or as a sophisticated side dish at any BBQ or dinner party.

SERVES 4

PREP TIME 10 MIN.	COOK TIME 30 MIN.	TOTAL TIME 40 MIN.

1 cup (240ml) balsamic vinegar

2 large organic sweet potatoes (~453g or 1 lb), sliced into thick wedges, skin on

2 Tbsp (30ml) grape seed oil, avocado oil, or coconut oil

¼ tsp sea salt, plus more to taste

1 cup (100g) raw pecans

¾ tsp ground cumin

¾ tsp ground cinnamon

1-2 Tbsp (12-24g) coconut sugar

¼ cup (43g) pomegranate arils*

OPTIONAL
Pinch of cayenne pepper

¼ cup (15g) chopped fresh parsley

01 Preheat the oven to 400 degrees F (204 degrees C) and grease two large rimmed baking sheets.

02 In the meantime, place the vinegar in a small saucepan. Bring to a low boil over medium heat. Then reduce the heat to medium-low and simmer until reduced by half, about 20 minutes. It's done when a spatula leaves a line when you run it across the bottom of the pan. Once it cools, it will thicken even more. Set aside.

03 While the balsamic vinegar cooks, spread the sweet potato wedges onto the prepared baking sheets. Toss with the grape seed oil and a pinch of salt, then spread into an even layer.

04 Bake for a total of 25-30 minutes, or until golden brown and tender. Flip at the halfway point to ensure even cooking.

05 In the meantime, prepare the nut topping. Add the pecans to the bowl of a food processor or blender and process into a fine meal. Add to a large skillet over medium heat, then add the cumin, cinnamon, sugar, ¼ tsp salt, and the coconut sugar. Stir to combine. Continue cooking until the mixture is golden brown and fragrant,

8-10 minutes, stirring frequently. Be careful not to burn. Taste and adjust the seasonings as needed. Set aside.

06 To serve, arrange the sweet potato wedges on a serving platter. Drizzle with balsamic glaze, pomegranate arils, and spiced nut topping (you will have leftovers*). Garnish with cayenne and fresh parsley (optional). Best when fresh.

Notes

*Pomegranate arils are the gorgeous magenta seeds inside the fruit. To extract, halve pomegranate and immerse in a bowl of cool water. Then gently break apart and use your hands to "pop" out the arils. The arils will sink to the bottom, and the white pieces and skin will float to the top. Use your hands to sort through arils and pick away any unwanted fragments or underripe arils.

*Store leftover nut topping in a secure jar at room temperature for up to 1 month. Great for topping oatmeal, pancakes, salads, and more.

THAI QUINOA MEATBALLS, PAGE 171

Main Dishes

THE MAIN EVENT.

These meals are meant to nourish, satisfy, satiate, and wow you.
I hope they do all of these things. I've worked hard to help keep
your dinner table full and your guests happy.

Need a place to start? How about the Thai Quinoa Meatballs (page
171) and Pizza Burgers (page 181)? Then move on to The Trashy Vegan
Sandwich (page 168)—it's become somewhat of a staple in our house.
Use these delicious entrées to feed your family, your friends, and,
of course, the occasional stranger. Nothing would make me happier.

White Bean Posole Verde

Posole always intimidated me with the complex cooking methods it requires, but this 10-ingredient version keeps things simple without sacrificing on flavor. Roasted tomatillos, jalapeños, and poblano peppers create a rich base with a beautiful green hue, while white beans add buttery texture and added protein and fiber. Serve this spicy soup with tortilla chips, fresh lime juice, and ripe avocado for added creaminess.

SERVES 4

PREP TIME 10 MIN. | **COOK TIME 45 MIN.** | **TOTAL TIME 55 MIN.**

2 poblano peppers (35g)

¾ pound (340g) tomatillos, outer husk removed

1-2 jalapeños, depending on preferred heat

2 Tbsp (30ml) olive oil or grape seed oil

4 cloves garlic (2 Tbsp or 12g), minced

½ medium white or yellow onion (55g), diced

4 cups (960ml) vegetable broth

1 15-ounce (425g) can white or butter beans, rinsed and drained

1 15-ounce (425g) can hominy or yellow corn, drained

Sea salt and black pepper, to taste

TOPPINGS (*optional*)
Lime juice

Tortilla chips

Ripe avocado, cubed

Fresh cilantro, chopped

Pomegranate seeds or thinly sliced radish

01 Preheat the oven to high broil and position a rack at the top of the oven.

02 Place the whole poblano peppers, tomatillos, and jalapeños (use one for less heat) on a rimmed baking sheet and, once the oven is hot, broil on high until charred on the top side. Then flip over and continue broiling until the other side is blackened. (The tomatillos will likely take longer, so remove the peppers from the oven once they are charred and continue roasting the tomatillos until blackened on the top and bottom.)

03 While the peppers are roasting, heat a large pot or saucepan over medium heat.

04 Once the saucepan is hot, add the olive oil, garlic, and onion. Sauté, stirring frequently, until soft and translucent and slightly browned, 4-5 minutes. Once done, add to the bowl of a blender (or, if using an immersion blender, remove from the heat and leave in the pot.)

05 Remove the charred peppers and tomatillos from the oven and wrap the peppers in foil to steam.

06 Wait 3 minutes, then remove the skin, core, and seeds from the poblanos and jalapeños and any stems from the tomatillos.

continued

07 Add to a blender with the garlic and onion. Blend/purée until the consistency is semi-fine. A little chunkiness is OK and even good (depending on your texture preference).

08 Add the mixture back to the pot over medium heat. Add the broth, beans, and hominy and stir.

09 Bring to a simmer, then cover, reduce the heat to low, and continue simmering until the beans have absorbed the flavor of the broth, at least 15 minutes. The longer it cooks, the more flavorful it will become.

10 Sample and adjust the seasonings as needed. Serve as is, or with desired toppings.

11 Store leftovers in the refrigerator for 4-5 days, or in the freezer up to 1 month.

Super-Thick Three-Bean Chili

This 1-pot meal is everything I look for in a veggie chili. It's hearty, well spiced, and thick in texture. This is a great dish to make ahead for quick, weeknight meals, or for entertaining in the fall and winter months. Hot sauce, avocado, and tortilla chips make the perfect garnish.

SERVES 6

PREP TIME 15 MIN. | **COOK TIME 45 MIN.** | **TOTAL TIME 60 MIN.**

1 Tbsp (15ml) grape seed oil, avocado oil, or coconut oil

½ white onion (55g), diced

1 clove garlic (3g), minced

1-2 tsp sea salt, or to taste

1 tsp black pepper

½ cup (64g) diced carrots

1 green bell pepper (119g), diced

2 large or 3 small sweet potatoes (~390g), diced with skin on

1 cup (124g) chopped zucchini squash

2 Tbsp (16g) chili powder

1 Tbsp (8g) ground cumin

1½ tsp garlic powder

1½ tsp smoked paprika

1 15-ounce (425g) can black beans, slightly drained

01 Heat a large pot over medium heat. Once hot, add the grape seed oil, onion, and garlic. Season with a pinch each of salt and pepper. Stir.

02 Cook for 4-5 minutes, or until the onion is soft, translucent, and slightly golden brown. Reduce the heat if browning too quickly.

03 Add the carrots, bell pepper, sweet potatoes, and zucchini. Season again with a healthy pinch of each salt and pepper (be generous), followed by the chili powder, cumin, garlic powder, and paprika.

04 Stir to coat. Cook over medium heat for 3-4 minutes to let flavors infuse and cook the vegetables.

05 Next add the black beans, pinto beans, chickpeas, tomatoes, tomato sauce, broth, maple syrup, and hot sauce (optional). Stir.

06 Bring the chili to a low boil, then reduce the heat to low and simmer. Add the drained corn and stir. Cover and cook for at least 30 minutes, or until thick and all of the vegetables are tender. The longer it simmers, the richer and thicker it will become.

continued

1 15-ounce (425g) can
pinto beans, slightly
drained

1 15-ounce (425g) can
chickpeas, well rinsed
and drained

1 15-ounce (425g)
can diced tomatoes in
juice (if unsalted, add
more salt)

½ cup (122g) tomato sauce
[or ¼ cup (66g) tomato
paste, plus ⅓ cup water]

2½ cups (600ml) vegetable
broth

2-3 Tbsp (30-45ml) maple
syrup or agave nectar (or
substitute coconut sugar)

1 Tbsp (15ml) hot sauce
(optional)

1 15-ounce (425g) can
whole kernel corn,
drained

FOR SERVING
Tortilla chips

Hot sauce or salsa

Ripe avocado, sliced

Fresh cilantro, chopped

07 Taste and adjust the seasonings as
needed. I add more chili powder and cumin
for heat, and sweetener to balance the
flavors.

08 Serve hot with recommended toppings.
Leftovers will keep covered in the
refrigerator for 4-5 days, or in the
freezer up to 1 month.

Cornbread Chili Potpies

When I was growing up, my grade-school cafeteria served the absolute best homemade chili. It was a full-on race to be at the front of the line to get the first serving. This dish combines my Super-Thick Three-Bean Chili and my favorite classic vegan cornbread from the blog. The result is a potpie-inspired meal that is savory, sweet, and seriously delicious. Hello, comfort food!

SERVES 6 TO 8

PREP TIME 15 MIN. | COOK TIME 35 MIN. | TOTAL TIME 50 MIN.

1½ Flax Eggs (see Flax Egg, page 6)

¾ cup plus 1 Tbsp (195ml) unsweetened plain almond milk or DIY Almond Milk (page 6)

1 tsp freshly squeezed lemon juice or vinegar

½ teaspoon baking soda

⅓ cup (74g) vegan butter, melted

½ cup (100g) organic cane sugar or organic granulated sugar

2 Tbsp (30g) unsweetened applesauce

½ tsp sea salt

¾ cup plus 1 Tbsp (108g) fine yellow cornmeal

¾ cup plus 1 Tbsp (110g) unbleached all-purpose flour

4½ cups (~1,300g) Super-Thick Three-Bean Chili (page 120)

01 Preheat the oven to 350 degrees F (176 degrees C). Lightly grease 6 medium-sized ramekins (~3 inches wide at the base) or 8 small ramekins (~2 inches wide at the base). Place on a clean baking sheet. Set aside.

02 Prepare the flax eggs in a large bowl. Let sit for 5 minutes.

03 Measure out the almond milk in a liquid measuring cup. Add the lemon juice. Allow to curdle for 5 minutes, then add the baking soda. Stir once more. Set aside.

04 To the bowl with the flax eggs, add the melted butter and sugar. Whisk vigorously to combine. Then add the applesauce and whisk once more. Next add the almond milk mixture and whisk vigorously to combine.

05 Add the salt, cornmeal, and flour. Stir with a mixing spoon until just incorporated and no large lumps remain.

06 Fill the ramekins slightly less than three-fourths full with chili (cold or at room temperature), then top with the cornbread batter, being careful not to overfill. (*See note if you have leftover batter.)

07 Bake the potpies on a baking sheet, to catch spillover, for 32-38 minutes,

depending on the size of your ramekins, or until the edges of the cornbread are golden brown and the centers appear cooked through.

08 Remove from the oven and let cool 5-10 minutes before serving. Top with a bit of vegan butter and maple syrup, or a dash of hot sauce (optional). Best when fresh.

Note

*If there is leftover batter, bake in paper-lined or lightly greased muffin tins for 22-28 minutes at 350 degrees F (176 degrees C), or until a toothpick inserted into the center comes out clean. This should be done after potpies are finished baking.

Chickpea Fesenjan

We have been making fesenjan for dinner ever since John's aunt took us to a Persian restaurant in San Diego. We instantly fell in love with everything we ate. This dish is stew-like in texture with the perfect balance of savory and sweet. Chickpeas add healthy, plant-based fiber and protein. Enjoy it as a stew, or serve it atop rice—as we prefer it—for a more traditional approach.

SERVES 4

PREP TIME 10 MIN. | **COOK TIME 45 MIN.** | **TOTAL TIME 55 MIN.**

1½ cups (180g) raw walnuts

¼ cup (72ml) pomegranate molasses (or 1 cup or 236ml pomegranate juice)

2 Tbsp (30ml) olive oil, grape seed oil, or coconut oil

1 large yellow onion (150g), diced

¼ tsp each sea salt and black pepper, plus more as needed

1 15-ounce (425g) can chickpeas, well rinsed and drained

2 cups (480ml) vegetable broth

2-4 Tbsp (30-60ml) maple syrup or agave nectar (or substitute coconut sugar)

½ teaspoon each ground turmeric and ground cinnamon

Pinch of nutmeg (optional)

FOR SERVING (optional)
1 cup (180g) uncooked jasmine rice* (or subtitute Cauliflower Rice, page 8)

1 cup (187g) pomegranate arils

1 cup (60g) parsley, chopped

01 Preheat the oven to 350 degrees F (176 degrees C).

02 Add the walnuts to a rimmed baking sheet. Bake for 10 minutes.

03 If you are making pomegranate molasses from pomegranate juice, add the juice to a small saucepan and bring to a simmer over medium heat. Continue cooking for about 30 minutes, or until darkened in color and reduced to roughly ¼ cup (72ml). Reduce the heat to medium-low if bubbling too vigorously.

04 Once the walnuts are finished roasting, let them cool slightly, then add to the bowl of a food processor or high-speed blender and pulse into a fine meal. Set aside.

05 Heat an extra-large skillet or pot over medium heat and add the olive oil and onion. Season with a pinch each of salt and pepper and stir. Cook for 4-5 minutes, or until soft and translucent.

06 Add the chickpeas, broth, walnut meal, pomegranate molasses, maple syrup, turmeric, cinnamon, ¼ tsp salt ¼ tsp pepper, and nutmeg, if using. Stir to combine and bring to a simmer. Reduce the heat to low and continue simmering for 10-15 minutes, or until thick and fragrant. Stir occasionally. Taste and adjust seasonings as needed.

07 Serve fesenjan over cooked rice* and garnish with pomegranate arils and fresh chopped parsley (optional), or enjoy as a stew.

08 Leftovers keep well, covered in the refrigerator, for 3-4 days, though best when fresh.

Notes

*Prepare jasmine rice while the walnuts are roasting. Bring 1 cup (180g) rice and 2 cups (480ml) water to a boil in a large saucepan. Then reduce the heat, cover, and simmer 15-20 minutes or until fluffy. Check the package to verify the instructions, which can vary depending on the type of rice.

*A green salad makes an excellent side to this flavorful dish, as does pita bread.

Simple Curried Carrot + Lentil Soup

This 1–pot curry soup is robust with curry flavor and super-creamy thanks to coconut milk. The lentils add tons of protein, iron, and fiber, making this a satisfying and wholesome plant-based meal. Though it stands up on its own, this soup is also delicious alongside Indian entrées.

SERVES 4

PREP TIME 10 MIN.	COOK TIME 50 MIN.	TOTAL TIME 60 MIN.

2 Tbsp (30ml) coconut oil

½ medium white or yellow onion (55g), diced

4 cloves garlic (2 Tbsp or 12g), minced

1 cup (128g) finely diced carrots

¼ tsp each sea salt and black pepper, plus more to taste

3 Tbsp (45g) green curry paste

1 cup (192g) dry green lentils, rinsed in a fine-mesh strainer

3 cups (720ml) vegetable broth, plus more as needed

1 cup (236ml) light coconut milk, plus more as needed

3 Tbsp (45ml) maple syrup (or substitute coconut sugar), plus more to taste

1 tsp ground turmeric, plus more to taste

01 Heat a large pot over medium heat. Once hot, add the coconut oil, onion, garlic, and carrot. Season with salt and pepper. Continue cooking, stirring frequently, until the onion is translucent and slightly browned, 4-5 minutes.

02 Add the curry paste and stir. Then add the lentils and stir once more.

03 Add the broth, coconut milk, maple syrup, and turmeric. Bring to a boil over high heat. Once boiling, reduce the heat to low and cover. Simmer for 30-45 minutes, or until the lentils are tender. If the soup becomes too thick, add more coconut milk or broth to thin.

04 Taste and adjust the seasonings as needed, adding more salt, pepper, turmeric, or sweetener as needed.

05 OPTIONAL: For creamier texture, scoop out half the soup and purée in a blender until creamy and smooth. (Or, purée with an immersion blender in the pot for similar results.) Add back to pot and stir.

06 Serve as is, or with fresh cilantro, sliced green onion, lemon or lime juice, and/or pomegranate arils. Leftovers will keep covered in the refrigerator for up to 5 days, or in the freezer for up to 1 month.

Masala Chickpea Curry

If you haven't figured it out yet, I'm a rather big fan of chickpeas and curry. This dish highlights both ingredients beautifully. The sauce is creamy and rich, thanks to blended carrots and coconut milk. A masala spice blend imparts tons of bold flavor, and the chickpeas add a crispy finishing touch. Serve this over rice for one delicious plant-based meal.

SERVES 4

PREP TIME 5 MIN. | **COOK TIME 25 MIN.** | **TOTAL TIME 30 MIN.**

2½ Tbsp (37ml) coconut oil

½ medium white or yellow onion (55g), diced

5 cloves garlic (2½ Tbsp or 15g), minced

1 Tbsp (6g) finely grated ginger

1½ cups (192g) finely diced carrots

¼ tsp each sea salt and black pepper, plus more to taste

4 Tbsp (32g) garam masala spice blend*

1 cup (236ml) light coconut milk

1 cup (240ml) vegetable broth

2-3 Tbsp (30-45ml) maple syrup (or substitute coconut sugar), to taste

1 15-ounce (425g) can chickpeas, rinsed and drained

continued

01 If serving with rice, cook the rice according to the package instructions and set aside, covered.

02 In the meantime, heat a large pot or saucepan over medium heat. Once hot, add 2 Tbsp of the coconut oil, the onion, garlic, ginger, and carrot. Season with ¼ tsp each salt and pepper. Stir to coat.

03 Cover and cook for 4-5 minutes, or until the carrots are slightly tender and the onion is translucent, stirring frequently.

04 Add 2½ Tbsp (20g) of the garam masala spice blend. Stir to coat. Then add the coconut milk, broth, and maple syrup. Bring to a simmer. Then lower the heat and cover once more. Cook for 5 minutes.

05 Transfer the mixture to the bowl of a blender or food processor and purée into a smooth, creamy sauce, scraping down the sides as needed. Taste and adjust the seasonings, adding more salt, pepper, or maple syrup as desired.

06 With the sauce still in the blender, add the chickpeas to the same pot from earlier with remaining ½ Tbsp coconut oil. Cook over medium heat.

continued

FOR SERVING (*optional*)
3 cups (474g) cooked rice, quinoa, or Cauliflower Rice (page 8)

Fresh cilantro, parsley, or mint, chopped

Freshly squeezed lime or lemon juice

07 Add the remaining 1½ Tbsp (12g) of the garam masala spice blend and a generous pinch of sea salt.

08 Cook for 3 minutes, then scoop out ½ cup (92g) of the chickpeas to reserve for the topping.

09 Add the curry sauce back into the pot with the chickpeas and simmer, covered, for another 10-15 minutes (up to 20-30 minutes). The longer the curry sauce simmers, the richer the flavor of the sauce and chickpeas. In the meantime, prepare any desired toppings.

10 To serve, top the rice with the curry and the reserved chickpeas. The flavor in this dish is elevated by fresh lime or lemon juice and fresh herbs, so I highly recommend them as a finishing touch.

11 Leftovers keep well for 2-3 days covered, in the refrigerator, though best when fresh. Freeze for up to 1 month.

Note

*DIY Garam Masala Spice Blend: Combine 3 Tbsp (24g) cumin, 2 Tbsp (16g) garlic powder, 2 Tbsp (16g) paprika, 2 tsp coriander, 2 tsp cardamom, 1 tsp cinnamon, ½ tsp ground cloves, and a pinch of cayenne or red chili powder.

Carrot, Potato + Chickpea Red Curry

This vegetable-based tomato red curry is loaded with rich curry flavor without being too spicy. It's so hearty when served over rice that it's easily a meal in itself. Serve this to vegans and meat-eaters alike and watch them clean their plates. Chili-spiced mango makes an excellent side dish.

SERVES 4

PREP TIME 10 MIN. | **COOK TIME 35 MIN.** | **TOTAL TIME 45 MIN.**

2 Tbsp (30ml) olive oil, grape seed oil, or coconut oil

3 cloves garlic (1½ Tbsp or 9g), minced

½ medium white or yellow onion (55g), diced

1½ cups (192g) coarsely chopped carrots

6 red or yellow baby potatoes, cut into bite-size wedges

Healthy pinch each of sea salt and black pepper, plus more to taste

1 15-ounce (425g) can chickpeas, thoroughly rinsed and drained

¼ cup (80g) red curry paste, plus more to taste

1 6-ounce (170g) can tomato paste

1½ cups (360ml) vegetable broth

1 cup (240ml) water

continued

01 Heat a large pot over medium heat. Once hot, add the olive oil, garlic, onion, carrots, and potatoes. Season with the salt and pepper. Cover and cook for 4 minutes.

02 Add chickpeas and curry paste. Stir to coat. Cook for 2 minutes more, then remove from the heat.

03 Add tomato paste, broth, water, coconut sugar, and turmeric. Stir to combine. Place back over medium heat and cover. The liquid should barely cover all of the ingredients, so add more water if needed.

04 Once the mixture has reached a simmer, reduce the heat to low and continue simmering, covered, for 20-25 minutes, or until the potatoes are fork tender and the flavor has permeated the chickpeas and vegetables.

05 While the curry is cooking, prepare any side dishes or toppings you wish, such as basmati rice, Cauliflower Rice, or Quick-Pickled Onions.

06 Taste and adjust the seasonings as needed, adding more curry paste for depth of flavor and heat, salt, or coconut sugar for sweetness.

continued

2 Tbsp (24g) coconut
sugar (or substitute
organic cane sugar or
maple syrup), plus more
to taste

½ tsp ground turmeric

FOR SERVING *(optional)*
Quick-Pickled Onions
(page 11)

3 cups cooked basmati
rice or Cauliflower Rice
(page 8)

Fresh chopped cilantro
or parsley

Sliced ripe mango with
chili powder

07 Serve as is or with desired toppings
or sides. Leftovers will stay fresh in
the refrigerator for 3-4 days, or in the
freezer for up to 1 month. Best when fresh.

1-Pot Chickpea Noodle Soup

Everyone needs a good, homemade noodle soup in their arsenal, especially when some-one in the household is under the weather. Carrots and celery add bursts of color and fiber, gluten-free noodles and chickpeas add protein and texture, and thyme and bay leaf marry all of the flavors together. Cozy up to a bowl of this simple, 1-pot, plant-based soup.

SERVES 6

PREP TIME 10 MIN. | COOK TIME 50 MIN. | TOTAL TIME 60 MIN.

½ medium white or yellow onion (~55g), diced

4 cloves garlic (2 Tbsp or 12g), coarsely chopped

2 Tbsp (30ml) olive oil, grape seed oil, or avocado oil

5 whole carrots (305g), scrubbed clean and coarsely chopped

4 stalks celery (160g), coarsely chopped

¼ tsp each sea salt and black pepper, plus more to taste

7-8 cups (1,680-1,920 ml) vegetable broth (depending on desired thickness)

1 15-ounce (425g) can chickpeas, well rinsed and drained

4 sprigs thyme

8 ounces (227g) gluten-free vegan spaghetti noodles (or any shape)

OPTIONAL
1 bay leaf

01 In a large pot over medium heat, sauté the onion and garlic in the olive oil for 5 minutes, stirring frequently.

02 Add the carrots, celery, salt, and pepper. Stir. Cover and cook for 5 minutes, stirring occasionally.

03 Add the broth, chickpeas, thyme, and bay leaf (optional). Bring to a low boil. Add the noodles—break them into smaller pieces for bite-size noodles. Stir occasionally while cooking to prevent the noodles from sticking together.

04 Once the noodles are soft, about 10 minutes, reduce the heat to low and cover. Continue simmering for 20-30 minutes to meld the flavors.

05 Taste and adjust the seasonings as needed. Remove the thyme sprigs and bay leaf and serve with rustic bread or as is. Thyme leaves make a colorful garnish.

06 Store leftovers covered in the refrigerator for 3-4 days, or in the freezer for up to 1 month.

Butternut Squash, Kale + Quinoa Bake

This simple, 10-ingredient quinoa bake is an homage to everything I love about fall and winter: hearty produce and comfort food. Quinoa cooked in vegetable broth is rich with flavor, the roasted butternut squash and mushrooms add heartiness and warmth, and the kale adds nutrition and bursts of color. Enjoy this as an entrée or side dish, especially during the holidays.

SERVES 6 | **PREP TIME 20 MIN.** | **COOK TIME 35 MIN.** | **TOTAL TIME 55 MIN.**

3 cups (420g) butternut squash chopped into small, bite-size cubes (see note)

2 Tbsp (30ml) grape seed oil or avocado oil

Sea salt and black pepper, to taste

¾ cup (138g) white quinoa

1½ cups (360ml) vegetable broth

½ medium yellow onion (55g), sliced into thin rings

2 cloves garlic (1 Tbsp or 6g), minced

8 ounces (227g) crimini, button, or baby bella mushrooms, quartered

½ cup (60g) walnuts, coarsely chopped (optional)

3 cups loosely packed (200g) kale, chopped

⅓ cup (26g) Vegan Parmesan (page 7)

01 Lightly grease an 8 × 8-inch (or comparable size) baking dish and preheat the oven to 400 degrees F (204 degrees C).

02 Line a rimmed baking sheet with foil or parchment paper. Add the cubed butternut squash and 1 Tbsp (15ml) grape seed oil. Season with a healthy pinch each of salt and pepper.

03 Toss to coat and bake for 12-14 minutes, or until just fork tender. Remove from the heat and set aside.

04 In the meantime, thoroughly rinse quinoa in a fine-mesh strainer. Add it to a small saucepan with the broth and bring to a boil over high heat, then reduce the heat to low and cover. Cook until the liquid is fully absorbed and the quinoa is fork tender, about 15 minutes. Set aside, covered.

05 Heat a large skillet over medium heat. Once hot, add the remaining 1 Tbsp (15ml) grape seed oil, onion, and garlic. Season with a pinch each of salt and pepper.

06 Cook until the onion is soft and translucent, 4-5 minutes, stirring frequently. Add the mushrooms and walnuts (optional) and season once more with salt and pepper. Continue cooking for 5 minutes, or until the mushrooms are lightly browned.

continued

07 Make room in the pan and add the kale. Season once more with salt and pepper and stir to coat. Cook until the kale is just tender, about 3 minutes. Remove from the heat and set aside.

08 Once quinoa is finished cooking, season with a healthy pinch each of salt and pepper and half of the Vegan Parmesan. Stir, sample, and adjust the seasonings to taste. Remove from the heat and set aside to rest.

09 Reduce the oven temperature to 375 degrees F (190 degrees C) and add the cooked quinoa to the prepared baking dish. Top with the vegetable-walnut mixture and roasted butternut squash. Lightly stir/toss to combine.

10 Top with the remaining 2-3 Tbsp (10-15g) Vegan Parmesan and bake uncovered for 5-7 minutes to warm through. Serve immediately.

11 Leftovers will keep, covered, for up to 3 days, though best when fresh.

Note

*The best way to cube butternut squash is to start with a large, very sharp knife, cutting off the top and bottom portions. Then cut in half where the small, cylinder shape and round, bulb-shape meet. Use a knife to carefully remove the skin. Then remove any seeds with a spoon. Cut into small cubes and proceed with the recipe as directed.

Roasted Chickpea Tabbouleh Salad

Tabbouleh is one of my favorite side dishes when we eat Mediterranean food. I love the bright lemon flavor and vibrant green color of the parsley. This version is upgraded to an entrée with the addition of crispy, baked chickpeas. Enjoy as a stand-alone meal or alongside your favorite Mediterranean fare. Hummus makes an excellent pairing.

SERVES 2 AS ENTRÉE, 4 AS SIDE

PREP TIME 7 MIN. | **COOK TIME 23 MIN.** | **TOTAL TIME 30 MIN.**

CHICKPEAS

1 15-ounce (425g) can chickpeas, rinsed and drained

1 Tbsp (15ml) olive oil, grape seed oil, or avocado oil

1 tsp dried oregano

½ tsp ground cinnamon

1 tsp ground cumin

½ tsp each sea salt and black pepper

½ tsp smoked paprika (optional)

SALAD

3 cups packed (180g) minced fresh parsley

½ cup (55g) finely diced yellow onion

1 cup (150g) finely diced cherry tomatoes

3 Tbsp (45ml) olive oil

2 lemons, juiced (~4 Tbsp or 60ml)

Pinch each of sea salt and black pepper

DRESSING

¼ cup (60g) hummus (or substitute tahini)

continued

01 Preheat the oven to 375 degrees F (190 degrees C).

02 Toss the chickpeas in the olive oil, oregano, cinnamon, cumin, salt, pepper, and paprika (optional) and spread on a rimmed baking sheet. Bake for 20-23 minutes, or until roasted and golden brown. Set aside.

03 In the meantime, prepare the tabbouleh salad by adding the parsley, onion, and tomatoes to a medium bowl and dressing them with olive oil and lemon juice. Toss to coat, then taste and adjust the seasonings as desired, adding a pinch each of salt and pepper if needed.

04 Prepare the dressing by whisking together hummus or tahini, garlic, lemon juice, dill, and maple syrup. Add water or plain almond milk to thin into a pourable sauce. Taste and adjust seasonings as needed.

05 To serve, top the tabbouleh salad with the chickpeas (warm or room temperature) and dressing. Pita chips make excellent scoopers or garnish.

06 Best when fresh, though leftovers will keep in the refrigerator for 2-3 days. Store the chickpeas separate from the salad in an airtight container at room temperature.

2 cloves garlic
(1 Tbsp or 6g), minced

½ lemon, juiced
(1 Tbsp or 15ml)

½ tsp dried dill
(or 1½ tsp fresh dill)

1 Tbsp (15ml) maple
syrup or agave nectar

2-3 Tbsp (30-45ml) water,
unsweetened plain almond
milk, or DIY Almond Milk
(page 6)

Easy Weeknight Burrito Bowls

If you have a Chipotle addiction like we do, making your own burrito bowls at home can both save money and ensure everyone gets exactly what they want! This recipe is pretty simple in terms of concept, and it proves that you can make your own burrito bowls at home in just 30 minutes. Chips are optional. OK, let's be real. Chips are totally not optional.

SERVES 4

PREP TIME 5 MIN.	COOK TIME 25 MIN.	TOTAL TIME 30 MIN.

RICE
1 cup (200g) white rice uncooked (see note)

2 cups (480ml) water

¼ tsp sea salt

½ lime, juiced (1 Tbsp or 15ml)

2 Tbsp (8g) chopped cilantro

BLACK BEANS
1 15-ounce (425g) can black beans, slightly drained (if unsalted, add ¼ tsp salt) (see note)

¼ tsp each garlic powder, ground cumin, and chili powder

PEPPERS + ONIONS
1 Tbsp (15ml) grape seed oil, avocado oil, or coconut oil

1 green bell pepper (119g), seeds removed, thinly sliced

½ medium red onion (55g), thinly sliced

Pinch each of sea salt and black pepper

continued

01 Rinse the rice in a fine-mesh strainer. Add to a small saucepan with the water. Bring to boil over high heat, then cover, reduce heat to low, and simmer until the water is absorbed, 15-20 minutes. Do not lift the lid until it is finished cooking.

02 While the rice is cooking, add the black beans to a small or medium saucepan over medium heat. Bring to a simmer; add the garlic powder, cumin, and chili powder and stir. Then reduce the heat to low to keep warm until serving, stirring occasionally.

03 In the meantime, prepare the peppers and onions: Heat a large skillet over medium heat. Once hot, add the grape seed oil, bell pepper, onion, salt, and pepper. Sauté for 3-4 minutes, stirring frequently, or until tender and slightly browned. Set aside.

04 While peppers and onions are sautéing, add all of the corn salsa ingredients to a bowl and toss to combine. Taste and adjust the seasonings as needed. Set aside.

05 Last, add all of the guacamole ingredients to a small bowl. Mash to combine using a fork or potato masher. Taste and adjust the seasonings as needed.

continued

CORN SALSA (see note)

1 cup (150g) corn, fresh or canned

¼ cup (37g) finely diced tomatoes

1 jalapeño (14g), seeds removed and finely diced

¼ cup (27g) finely diced red onion

½ lime, juiced
(1 Tbsp or 15ml)

1 Tbsp (4g) chopped cilantro

Pinch each of sea salt and black pepper, plus more to taste

GUACAMOLE

1 ripe avocado

½ lime, juiced
(1 Tbsp or 15ml)

Pinch each of sea salt and black pepper, plus more to taste

1 Tbsp (4g) chopped cilantro

06 Once finished cooking, remove the rice from the heat. Add the salt, lime juice, and cilantro.

07 To serve, scoop the rice into serving bowls and top with beans, peppers and onions, corn salsa, guacamole, and any other desired toppings. I love extra red salsa, hot sauce, and tortilla chips.

08 Store leftovers separately (covered) in the refrigerator for 3-4 days. Corn salsa will keep 5-7 days.

Notes

*I like using white rice because it cooks much faster and keeps this recipe under 30 minutes. But you can substitute brown rice if you prefer.

*To switch it up, substitute vegan refried beans or pinto beans for black beans.

*Instead of the corn salsa, you can also substitute your favorite red or green salsa.

Garlic Pineapple Stir-Fried Quinoa

Stir-fried rice is one of my favorite Asian dishes. However, it's not always the healthiest, so I swapped in quinoa for added protein and nutritional value. I borrowed the cashew and pineapple idea from my college roommate, who made some of the best fried rice. The 5-ingredient sauce melds everything together to create a flavorful, hearty entrée or side dish.

SERVES 4

PREP TIME 10 MIN. | **COOK TIME 10 MIN.** | **TOTAL TIME 20 MIN.***

STIR-FRY

1¼ cups (212g) uncooked quinoa, rinsed*

2½ cups (600ml) water

1 Tbsp (15ml) toasted sesame oil or coconut oil

1 cup (87g) diced green onion

3 cloves garlic (1½ Tbsp or 9g), minced

½ cup (63g) peas, fresh or frozen

⅔ cup (80g) roasted salted cashews

⅔ cup (110g) diced pineapple

SAUCE

1 Tbsp (15ml) toasted sesame oil

¼ cup (60ml) soy sauce or tamari

4-5 Tbsp (60-75ml) maple syrup (or substitute organic brown sugar)

3 cloves garlic (1½ Tbsp or 9g), minced

3-4 Tbsp (48-64g) salted natural peanut butter, cashew butter, or almond butter

01 Add the quinoa and water to a large saucepan. Cook over high heat until boiling, then reduce the heat to low. Cover and simmer until liquid is absorbed, about 15 minutes. Set aside.

02 Whisk all of the sauce ingredients together in a small bowl and set aside.

03 Heat a large skillet over medium heat. Once hot, add the sesame oil, green onion, garlic, and 1 Tbsp (15ml) sauce. Sauté for 1-2 minutes, then add the peas. Cook for another 2 minutes. Raise the heat to medium. Add the cooked quinoa and two-thirds of the sauce (reserving the rest for serving). Stir to thoroughly coat. Cook for 1-2 minutes.

04 Add the cashews and pineapple. Stir to coat. Cook for another 1-2 minutes, stirring frequently.

05 Serve with the remaining sauce on the side. Chopped green onion or cilantro makes a colorful garnish. Best when fresh, though leftovers will keep, covered, in the refrigerator for 3-4 days.

Note

*Total time does not include cooking the quinoa.

Cashew Soba Noodle Salad

Soba noodles are an ingredient I feel are still on the fringe of food popularity, but they belong in the spotlight! They're quick, easy to make, and absorb any sauce they are covered in. This noodle salad is packed with protein and healthy fats from shelled edamame and cashews. Mangoes add a burst of color and hint of sweetness to this 30-minute, plant-based meal.

SERVES 2 AS ENTRÉE, 4 AS SIDE

PREP TIME 20 MIN. | **COOK TIME 10 MIN.** | **TOTAL TIME 30 MIN.**

5 ounces (141g) soba noodles (substitute rice noodles if gluten-free)

1 cup (155g) shelled edamame

1 cup (128g) thinly sliced carrots

1 red bell pepper (119g), thinly sliced

½ cup (80g) snow or sugar snap peas, chopped in half

¼ cup (15g) chopped cilantro

¼ cup (30g) roasted salted cashews, chopped, plus more for serving

1 mango, peeled and chopped into bite-size pieces

1 lime, sliced, for garnish

CASHEW GINGER DRESSING
½ cup (128g) salted creamy cashew butter (or substitute almond or peanut butter—if unsalted, add additional soy sauce)

2 Tbsp (30ml) tamari or soy sauce, plus more for dressing the noodles

¾ tsp chili garlic sauce

01 Cook the soba noodles according to package instructions. Then drain, rinse with cool water, and set aside.

02 While the noodles are cooking, prepare the vegetables. To cook the edamame, microwave for 1 minute, covered. Or add to a saucepan over medium-low heat with 1-2 Tbsp (15-30ml) water, cover, and cook until warmed through, about 2 minutes. Set aside.

03 To prepare the dressing, combine all of the ingredients (except the water) and whisk. Then add enough hot water to thin into a pourable sauce (~2-3 Tbsp or 30-45ml). Taste and adjust the seasonings as desired.

04 To serve, add all of the salad ingredients to a large bowl and toss with 1 Tbsp (15ml) soy sauce and 1 tsp toasted sesame oil. Then add the desired amount of dressing and serve at room temperature or chilled. Serve with chili garlic sauce for added heat and a few more roasted cashews for garnish (optional).

05 Leftovers will keep covered in the refrigerator for 2-3 days, though best when fresh.

2 Tbsp (30ml) maple syrup
or agave nectar (or
substitute coconut sugar)

½ lime, juiced
(1 Tbsp or 15ml)

1 tsp fresh grated ginger

1 tsp toasted sesame
oil, plus more for
dressing the noodles

Hot water to thin

Thai Baked Sweet Potatoes

My Mediterranean Baked Sweet Potatoes have become one of the most popular recipes on our blog, and this version takes the same concept and adds a Thai twist! Crispy, spiced chickpeas add plenty of protein and fiber, and the ginger-tahini sauce marries the dish together perfectly. This makes a great weeknight meal when you want something fast but delicious.

SERVES 4

PREP TIME 5 MIN. | **COOK TIME 25 MIN.** | **TOTAL TIME 30 MIN.**

4 medium (~1½ lbs or 680g) organic sweet potatoes, halved

1 Tbsp (15ml) grape seed oil

CHICKPEAS
1 15-ounce (425g) can chickpeas, drained

1 tsp garlic powder

1 tsp ground cumin

½ tsp ground or fresh ginger

¼ tsp ground coriander

1 Tbsp (15ml) maple syrup

1 Tbsp (15ml) soy sauce

½ tsp chili garlic sauce

½ Tbsp (8ml) coconut oil

GINGER TAHINI SAUCE
1 tsp fresh ginger, grated

¼ cup (56g) tahini (or peanut butter)

1 lime, juiced (2 Tbsp or 30ml)

1-2 Tbsp (15-30ml) soy sauce or tamari (if gluten-free, use tamari)

2-3 Tbsp (30-45ml) maple syrup (or substitute

continued

01 Preheat the oven to 400 degrees F (204 degrees C) and rub the halved sweet potatoes with the grape seed oil on all sides. Place on a foil-lined baking sheet and bake for 25 minutes (or more, depending on the size of the potato), or until very tender to the touch. Set aside.

02 In the meantime, heat a medium skillet over medium heat. In a small bowl, toss chickpeas with the garlic powder, cumin, ginger, coriander, maple syrup, soy sauce, and chili garlic sauce.

03 Once the skillet is hot, add the coconut oil. Sauté the chickpeas until visibly browned and slightly dried out, about 5 minutes. Set aside.

04 To prepare the sauce, add all of the ingredients (except the water) to the same bowl used for the chickpeas. Whisk to combine. Then add hot water to thin until pourable. Taste and adjust the seasonings as desired.

05 To serve, place the baked sweet potatoes on serving plates. Gently press into the middle of potatoes to make a well for the chickpeas. Add the chickpeas and top with the sauce and garnishes of choice.

06 Store leftovers (separately), covered, in the refrigerator for up to 3 days. Reheat in the microwave or a 350 degree F (176 degree C) oven until warmed through, about 20 minutes.

coconut sugar or organic
brown sugar)

½ tsp chili garlic sauce

Hot water to thin
(1-4 Tbsp or 15-60ml)

FOR GARNISH (optional)
2 green onions, diced

¼ cup (15g) cilantro,
finely chopped

½ lime, quartered

½ tsp chili garlic sauce

1 tsp sesame seeds
or crushed roasted,
salted peanuts

Spicy Tofu Vegetable Stir-Fry

If you've never marinated tofu, you are missing out on the easiest way to infuse big flavor into your meals. This simple sauce boasts bold flavor from soy sauce, chili garlic sauce, and toasted sesame oil. Fresh veggies make this a complete meal, which pairs perfectly with white rice, brown rice, or Cauliflower Rice (page 8). Serve with chili garlic sauce for extra heat.

SERVES 2	PREP TIME 2 HRS. 30 MIN.	COOK TIME 15 MIN.	TOTAL TIME 2 HRS. 45 MIN.

10 ounces (283g) extra-firm tofu

1 Tbsp (15ml) toasted sesame oil

3 cups (~350g) raw vegetables, chopped (broccoli, carrots, and/or cauliflower)

MARINADE
1-2 Tbsp (15-30g) chili garlic sauce (reduce for less heat)

¼ cup (60ml) maple syrup or agave nectar (or substitute coconut sugar)

¼ cup (60ml) tamari or soy sauce (if gluten-free, use tamari)

3 cloves garlic (1½ Tbsp or 9g), minced

1 lime, juiced (2 Tbsp or 30ml)

1 Tbsp (15ml) toasted sesame oil

1 Tbsp (8g) cornstarch or arrowroot starch, for thickening

01 Wrap the tofu in a clean, absorbent towel and set something heavy on top, such as a cast-iron skillet, to aid in absorbing excess moisture. Let rest for 15 minutes. Prepare the marinade at this time.

02 Add all of the marinade ingredients (except the cornstarch) to a plastic bag and toss/shake to combine. Once the tofu is pressed, cube it and add it to the marinade. Toss to combine.

03 Place in the refrigerator for at least 2 hours, preferably overnight (up to 2 days). The longer it rests, the stronger and more pronounced the flavor will become.

04 When ready to cook, heat a large skillet over medium heat. Once hot, add 1 Tbsp (15ml) sesame oil. Use a slotted spoon to scoop the tofu into the skillet, leaving the majority of the marinade behind.

05 Cook for 4-5 minutes, stirring frequently and adding 1-2 Tbsp (15-30 ml) marinade to add extra flavor. Flip/toss the tofu around to get all of the sides evenly browned. Reduce the heat if browning too quickly. Remove the pan from the heat and scoop out the tofu. Set aside (see note).

06 Add the cornstarch to the remaining marinade in the plastic bag. Toss the contents to thicken the sauce.

continued

07 Place the pan back over medium heat. Add the vegetables and remaining marinade. Sauté the vegetables, stirring frequently, for 1-2 minutes or until just tender. Then add the tofu back in and cook for 1-2 minutes more.

08 Serve as is or with white rice, brown rice, or Cauliflower Rice (page 8). Serve with extra chili garlic sauce for added heat.

09 Leftovers will keep stored in the refrigerator for up to 3 days. Reheat in the microwave or a skillet over medium heat until hot.

Note

*To further increase the firmness of the tofu after sautéing, add it to a parchment-lined baking sheet and bake at 400 degrees F (204 degrees C) for 20-30 minutes. Pause cooking the vegetables at this time, then proceed through the recipe as instructed.

Vegan Cobb Salad

Cobb salads have always been a favorite, but this vegan version takes the obsession to a whole new level. A bed of greens is topped with hearty ingredients including quinoa, avocado, chickpeas, and pecans for extra staying power. The balsamic vinaigrette is the perfect savory-sweet finish. Serve this as a stand-alone entrée or as a side dish to nearly any meal.

SERVES 2 AS ENTRÉE, 4 AS SIDE

PREP TIME 10 MIN. | **COOK TIME 20 MIN.** | **TOTAL TIME 30 MIN.**

½ cup (92g) quinoa, uncooked

½ Tbsp (7g) grape seed oil, avocado oil, or melted coconut oil

1 cup (240ml) vegetable broth or water

¼ medium red onion (15g), thinly sliced

1 ripe avocado (200g), chopped

1 cup (164g) cooked chickpeas, rinsed and drained well

4 cups (5 ounces or 141g) mixed greens or baby spinach

½ cup (75g) cherry tomatoes, halved

¼ cup (25g) roasted unsalted pecans (see note)

01 Rinse the quinoa thoroughly in a fine-mesh strainer. Add to a small saucepan over medium heat with the grape seed oil and toast for 2-3 minutes, stirring frequently.

02 Add the broth, bring to a boil, then reduce the heat to low, cover, and simmer for 15 minutes or until fluffy and the liquid is absorbed. Set aside.

03 Prepare the vegetables and chickpeas. Set aside.

04 To serve, add the greens to a large serving bowl or plate and top with the remaining salad ingredients (quinoa can be served warm or at room temperature).

05 Toss or serve with the dressing of your choice (see note). Store leftovers separate (covered) in the refrigerator for 2-3 days, though best when fresh.

Notes

*If the pecans are raw, roast them on a rimmed baking sheet for 10 minutes in a 350 degree F (176 degrees C) oven.

*In place of the Vegan Caesar Dressing pictured (recipe on page 110), you could opt for a simple balsamic vinaigrette: Add 3 Tbsp (45ml) balsamic vinegar, 2 tsp maple syrup, a pinch each of sea salt and black pepper, and ⅓ cup (80ml) olive oil to a mason jar (or small bowl) and shake vigorously (or whisk) to combine.

Better-Than-Restaurant Vegan Nachos

I have created one version of vegan nachos on the blog but wanted to upgrade it with my Best Ever 20-minute Vegan Queso, which does a stand-up job of mocking the flavor, texture, and mouthfeel of real cheese sauce! Toppings are versatile and plenty, and if you bake your own chips, this is actually a pretty healthy snack or meal.

SERVES 4

PREP TIME 10 MIN. | **COOK TIME 20 MIN.** | **TOTAL TIME 30 MIN.**

20 yellow corn tortillas, cut into small wedges (see note)

Nonstick cooking oil spray (for coating the tortillas)

½ tsp sea salt

1 cup (185g) black beans (if unsalted, season with salt to taste)

1 batch Best Ever 20-Minute Vegan Queso (page 73), warmed

¼ cup (34g) black olives, diced (optional)

PICO DE GALLO
¼ cup (15g) chopped cilantro

¼ cup (27g) diced red onion

½ cup (80g) diced tomato

1 lime, juiced (2 Tbsp or 30ml)

Pinch of sea salt

GUACAMOLE
1 ripe avocado

1 lime, juiced (2 Tbsp or 30ml)

Pinch of sea salt

01 Preheat the oven to 375 degrees F (190 degrees C) (skip this step if using store-bought chips). Spray (or brush) the tortillas with the nonstick cooking oil and season with salt. Toss to coat. Arrange on two baking sheets. Bake in batches for 10-12 minutes, flipping once halfway through to ensure even cooking. Set aside.

02 In the meantime, heat the black beans in a small saucepan over medium heat. Once simmering, reduce the heat to low to keep warm, stirring occasionally.

03 Prepare the pico de gallo by adding all of the ingredients to a small bowl. Toss to combine.

04 Add the guacamole ingredients to a small bowl. Mash to combine. Taste and adjust the flavor.

05 To serve, add the chips to a large serving platter and top with queso, black beans, black olives (optional), pico de gallo, guacamole, and any other desired toppings, such as cilantro, salsa, or hot sauce.

Note

*To save time, use 5-6 cups store-bought tortilla chips in place of the corn tortillas.

Spicy Braised Tofu Tostadas

This recipe is inspired by the Sofritas tofu at Chipotle! If you don't think you are a tofu fan, this recipe is determined to change your mind. It's packed with smoky Southwest flavor; has tons of peppers, onions, and tomatoes; and comes together in just 30 minutes. Enjoy it on burrito bowls, tacos, nachos, or atop crispy tostadas as I have done here.

SERVES 3 (YIELDS 6 TOSTADAS)

PREP TIME 5 MIN. | **COOK TIME 25 MIN.** | **TOTAL TIME 30 MIN.**

2 Tbsp (30ml) grape seed oil or avocado oil

5 cloves garlic (3½ Tbsp or 15g), minced

¼ white or yellow onion (55g), diced

½ green or red bell pepper (60g), diced

¼ tsp each sea salt and black pepper, plus more to taste

10 ounces (283g) extra-firm tofu, patted dry and crumbled with a fork

1½ tsp chili powder

1½ tsp ground cumin

1 tsp garlic powder

1 chipotle pepper in adobo sauce, chopped, plus 1 tsp adobo sauce (optional)

1 cup (240ml) vegetable broth

½ cup (~128g) red salsa

TOSTADAS

6 white or yellow corn tortillas

continued

01 Heat a large skillet over medium heat. Once hot, add the grape seed oil, garlic, onion, and bell pepper. Season with a pinch each of salt and pepper. Cook for 3-4 minutes, stirring frequently until the onion is translucent and the bell peppers are lightly browned.

02 Raise the heat to high and add the crumbled tofu. Cook for 5-6 minutes, stirring frequently, to begin browning. Then add the chili powder, cumin, and garlic powder. Stir to coat.

03 Add the chipotle pepper, adobo sauce (optional), broth, and salsa. Stir to combine, then reduce the heat to low, cover, and simmer for at least 15 minutes. The longer it simmers, the more flavor the tofu will absorb. Stir occasionally.

04 Prep any desired toppings at this time.

05 Just before serving, preheat the oven to low broil and position the oven rack at the top of the oven.

06 Brush the corn tortillas with the grape seed oil and arrange on 1 or 2 baking sheets, making sure they aren't crowded. Broil for 2-3 minutes on each side, or until light brown and crispy. Watch closely so they do not burn. Set aside.

continued

1-2 Tbsp (15-30ml) grape
seed oil or avocado oil
(for brushing)

TOPPINGS
Avocado (or guacamole)

Salsa of choice

Hot sauce

Red onion, diced

Cilantro, chopped

07 To serve, top the tostadas with braised
tofu and desired toppings. I love avocado,
lime juice, hot sauce, cilantro, and red
onion.

08 Braised tofu will keep covered in the
refrigerator for up to 5 days, though best
when fresh.

Note

*You can also enjoy the tofu in burritos, in
tacos, or atop salads.

The Best Vegan Enchiladas

The perfect vegan enchiladas had eluded me for years, but this version nails it. Corn tortillas remain tender with slightly crisp edges, a refried bean and poblano filling is hearty and simple, and the homemade enchilada sauce is rich and subtly spiced. Serve these to a crowd, or prepare as a quick and easy weeknight meal.

SERVES 4 (YIELDS 8 ENCHILADAS)

PREP TIME 15 MIN. | **COOK TIME 35 MIN.** | **TOTAL TIME 50 MIN.**

ENCHILADA SAUCE
1 Tbsp (15ml) grape seed oil, avocado oil, or coconut oil

½ large white onion (75g), diced

3 cloves garlic (1½ Tbsp or 9g), minced

1 15-ounce (425g) can tomato sauce

1 chipotle pepper in adobo (canned), chopped, plus 1 tsp adobo sauce (plus more for taste)

½ cup (120ml) water (or substitute vegetable broth)

1-2 Tbsp (15-30ml) maple syrup (or substitute coconut sugar), plus more to taste

Sea salt and black pepper, to taste

ENCHILADA FILLING
1 Tbsp (15ml) grape seed oil, avocado oil, or coconut oil

½ large white onion (75g), diced

continued

01 Heat a large skillet over medium heat. Once hot, add 1 Tbsp (15ml) grape seed oil, the onion, and the garlic. Cook, stirring frequently, until soft and translucent, 4-5 minutes.

02 Add the tomato sauce, chipotle pepper, adobo sauce (plus more to taste), maple syrup, and water. Reduce the heat to low and simmer for 5 minutes, covered (to prevent splattering).

03 Transfer the sauce to the bowl of a blender (optional) and blend well. Taste and adjust the seasonings as needed, adding more adobo sauce for heat, salt for savoriness, and maple syrup for sweetness.

04 Rinse the skillet slightly and place over medium heat to prepare the filling. Also preheat the oven to 350 degrees F (176 degrees C).

05 Once the skillet is hot, add 1 Tbsp (15ml) grape seed oil, the onion, and the poblano pepper. Season with the a pinch each of salt and pepper. Cook until the onion is translucent and the pepper has a bit of color, about 3-4 minutes.

06 Add the refried beans and stir/mash to combine. Add ⅓ cup (~90ml) of the enchilada sauce for extra flavor. Taste and adjust the seasonings as needed. Remove from the heat and set aside.

continued

1 poblano pepper (17g),
seeds removed, diced

Sea salt and black
pepper, to taste

1 15-ounce (425g) can
vegetarian refried beans
or pinto beans, well
drained

8 white or yellow corn
tortillas

TOPPINGS *(optional)*
Lime juice

Red onion, diced

Ripe avocado, sliced

Cilantro, torn/chopped

07 Wrap the tortillas in a damp paper
or cloth towel and microwave to warm for
30 seconds. (Alternatively, place the
tortillas directly on the oven rack for 1
minute to heat through.)

08 Pour a bit of sauce into the bottom of
9 × 13-inch (3-quart) baking dish. Spread
to coat. Take one corn tortilla and lay
it down in the dish. Fill with a modest
amount of filling (keeping in mind there
needs to be enough for 8-10 tortillas),
then roll up the tortilla. Place the seam-
side down at one end of the dish. Continue
until all of the tortillas are filled and
wrapped, adding more sauce as needed.

09 Pour the remaining sauce over the top
of the enchiladas in a stripe down the
middle. Brush/spray the edges with oil for
crisp edges (optional).

10 Bake at 350 degrees F (176 degrees C)
for 15-20 minutes, or until warmed through.
Top with desired toppings and serve.

11 I highly recommend lime juice,
red onion, avocado, and cilantro, but
these enchiladas are delicious on their
own! Leftovers keep, covered, in the
refrigerator for up to 3 days, though best
when fresh. Reheat in a 350 degree F (176
degree C) oven for 15-20 minutes, or until
warmed through.

Smashed Black Bean Green Chili Taquitos

Who says taquitos have to be junk food? These hearty snacks are filled with black beans and green chilies and achieve a crispy texture without frying! Serve with salsa or guacamole for an extra boost of flavor.

SERVES 4 (YIELDS 9–10 TAQUITOS) | **PREP TIME 10 MIN.** | **COOK TIME 25 MIN.** | **TOTAL TIME 35 MIN.**

1 Tbsp (15ml) olive oil, grape seed oil, or coconut oil plus more for brushing the taquitos

2 cloves garlic (1 Tbsp or 6g), minced

½ white or yellow onion (55g), diced

Healthy pinch each of sea salt and black pepper, plus more to taste

1 15-ounce (425g) can black beans, drained (not rinsed)

1 4-ounce (113g) can chopped mild green chilies, excess liquid drained

½ tsp ground cumin

¼ tsp chili powder

¼ cup (64g) chunky red salsa

9-10 yellow corn tortillas

FOR SERVING (optional)
Guacamole (see note)

Fresh lime juice

Salsa

01 Heat a large skillet over medium heat and preheat the oven to 425 degrees F (218 degrees C). Spray a baking sheet with nonstick spray or line with foil.

02 Once the skillet is hot, add the olive oil, garlic, and onion. Season with a pinch each of salt and pepper. Sauté until the onions are translucent and light brown, 4-5 minutes.

03 Add the black beans, green chilies, cumin, chili powder, salt, pepper, and red salsa. Stir to combine and use a wooden spoon or masher to smash most of the black beans so the filling becomes thicker and more cohesive.

04 Taste and adjust seasonings as needed. Cook for 2-3 minutes, then remove from the heat and set aside.

05 To make tortillas more pliable, warm in preheated oven for 30-45 seconds directly on the oven rack. Alternatively, wrap in a damp towel and microwave for 20-30 seconds.

06 Fill the tortillas one at a time with a small amount (2-3 Tbsp) of black bean/ green chili mixture. Roll into tight, cigar-like shape. Place seam-side down on the prepared baking sheet. Repeat until all of the filling is used, about 10

taquitos, depending on the size. Be sure to spread the taquitos out on baking sheet so they can brown on all sides.

07 Spray or brush generously with cooking spray or oil of choice—just make sure it has a high smoke point, such as grape seed oil or canola oil.

08 Bake for 14-17 minutes, or until crispy and golden brown. Serve immediately as is, or with salsa and guacamole. Best when fresh. See notes for freezing instructions.

Notes

*Find my go-to guacamole recipe in the Easy Weeknight Burrito Bowls recipe on page 141.

*To freeze for later use, partially bake the taquitos for 5 minutes and let cool. Then arrange them on a baking sheet and freeze until firm before packing in a freezer-safe container or bag. Reheat on a parchment-lined or lightly greased baking sheet at 425 degrees F (218 degrees C), until hot and golden brown, 15-20 minutes.

Vegan "No Tuna" Salad Sandwich

Inspired by my Chickpea Salad Sandwich from the blog, this "no-tuna" version gets extra tang and flavor from pickles and capers. Serve between two slices of your favorite hearty bread for a simple yet satisfying meal.

**YIELDS 2 CUPS
(MAKES 4 SANDWICHES)**

PREP TIME 10 MIN. | TOTAL TIME 10 MIN.

1 15-ounce (425g) can chickpeas, rinsed + drained

3 Tbsp (40g) vegan mayonnaise (see note)

1 Tbsp (14g) tahini

1 tsp Dijon or spicy mustard, plus more to taste

1 Tbsp (15ml) maple syrup or agave nectar, plus more to taste

¼ cup (15g) diced red onion

¼ cup (15g) diced celery

¼ cup (35g) diced pickle

1 tsp capers, drained and loosely chopped

Healthy pinch each of sea salt and black pepper, plus more to taste

1 Tbsp (7g) roasted unsalted sunflower seeds (optional)

FOR SERVING
8 slices wheat bread

Vegan mayonnaise

Deli mustard

Romaine lettuce

Tomato slices

Red onion, sliced

01 Add the chickpeas to a medium bowl and mash with a fork, leaving only a few beans whole.

02 Add the vegan mayonnaise, tahini, mustard, maple syrup, red onion, celery, pickle, capers, salt, pepper, and sunflower seeds (optional) to the bowl. Mix to incorporate. Taste and adjust the seasonings as needed. I add a bit more sweetener, salt, pepper, and mustard.

03 Toast the bread, if desired, and prepare any other desired sandwich toppings (such as lettuce, tomato, and onion).

04 Scoop a healthy amount of chickpea mixture (~½ cup) onto one slice of bread, add the desired toppings and sauce, and top with a second slice of bread. Repeat for additional sandwiches.

05 The mixture will keep, covered, in refrigerator for 4-5 days, making it great for quick, weekday lunches.

Note

*In place of mayonnaise, you can substitute 2-3 Tbsp (30-45g) additional tahini. Adjust the seasonings as needed.

The Trashy Vegan Sandwich

This recipe is inspired by my go-to order at Which Wich sandwich shop. Hearty slices of wheat bread are topped with hummus, avocado, caramelized onion, peppers, tomato, and a simple "no honey" mustard sauce. Alfalfa sprouts add nutrition and crunch, and a drizzle of Sriracha adds a wave of heat. This is my weekday lunch when I am craving something simple yet substantial.

SERVES 1

PREP TIME 15 MIN. | **COOK TIME 10 MIN.** | **TOTAL TIME 25 MIN.**

1 Tbsp (15ml) grape seed oil, avocado oil, or coconut oil

½ white or yellow onion (55g), sliced in thin rings

Pinch of sea salt

2 slices hearty wheat bread

2 tsp Dijon mustard (ensure vegan-friendly)

1 tsp maple syrup

¼ cup (60g) hummus

2-3 pepperoncinis, sliced, or banana peppers

2 tomato slices

¼ ripe avocado (~40g), sliced

¼ cup (8g) alfalfa sprouts or other greens of choice

1 Tbsp (15ml) hot sauce (such as Sriracha)

01 Heat a large skillet over medium heat. Once hot, add the grape seed oil and onion and stir. Season with the salt. Cook until soft, translucent, and caramelized, 8-10 minutes. Reduce the heat if browning too quickly and add 1 tsp water at a time if they are sticking to the pan. They should be very tender and sweet to the taste. Set aside.

02 Toast the bread if desired. While it's toasting, prep the other ingredients.

03 Combine the mustard and maple syrup in a small bowl and mix to combine. Add more mustard for a spicier spread, and more maple syrup for a sweeter spread.

04 To assemble the sandwich, spread hummus generously on bottom slice of bread. Top with caramelized onions, pepperoncinis, tomato, avocado, maple-Dijon sauce, alfalfa sprouts, and hot sauce.

05 Top with the second piece of bread and gently press down. Slice and serve immediately. Best when fresh.

Thai Quinoa Meatballs

Similar to my Thai Peanut Burgers (page 176), these "meatballs" are jam-packed with Thai-inspired flavors and come in a bite-size portion. Serve atop carrot noodles with peanut sauce for a hearty meal that's bursting with flavor.

SERVES 4 (YIELDS 23–25 MEATBALLS)

PREP TIME 20 MIN. | **COOK TIME 50 MIN.** | **TOTAL TIME 1 HR. 10 MIN.**

1 15-ounce (425g) can chickpeas, thoroughly rinsed, drained, and patted dry

½ cup (92g) cooked quinoa (see note)

¼ cup (55g) organic brown sugar (or substitute coconut sugar)

2 Tbsp (32g) salted peanut butter

2-3 Tbsp (30-45ml) tamari or soy sauce (if gluten-free, use tamari)

¼ cup (15g) finely chopped fresh cilantro, plus more for serving

¼ cup (38g) finely diced green onion

1 tsp chili garlic sauce

¾-1 cup (105-140g) roasted salted peanuts, crushed, plus more for coating and texture

FOR SERVING (optional)
6-8 whole carrots (366g), peeled and ribboned or thinly sliced

Peanut Sauce (page 10)

continued

01 Preheat the oven to 350 degrees F (176 degrees C). Arrange the chickpeas on a foil- or parchment-lined rimmed baking sheet. Bake for 12-13 minutes to dehydrate, then set aside. Keep the oven at 350 degrees F (176 degrees C).

02 Add the baked chickpeas to the bowl of a food processor or blender. Mix/pulse on low to pulverize. Alternatively, mash with a fork.

03 Add the chickpea mixture and remaining ingredients to a medium bowl. Stir/mix to combine. Taste and adjust the seasonings as needed. Add more crushed peanuts if too wet (bread crumbs work well here, too). I found 1 cup (~140g) to be the perfect amount. This will depend on how wet your quinoa and peanut butter are.

04 Scoop out amounts of dough slightly larger than 1 tablespoon. Gently roll into balls. Roll in additional crushed peanuts to coat.

05 Spray the foil-lined baking sheet used earlier with nonstick spray. Add the meatballs. Bake for 15 minutes, then gently turn/flip to ensure even cooking. Bake for another 10-15 minutes, or to desired doneness. The longer the meatballs

continued

Chili garlic sauce

Fresh cilantro, chopped

Lime juice

cook, the firmer they will get. Once they cool a little, they firm up even more.

06 While baking, prepare any additional serving items. To cook the carrots, bring a pot of water to a boil, add the ribboned carrots, and cook for 2-3 minutes or until just tender. Strain and set aside.

07 Serve the meatballs over carrot noodles with peanut sauce, chili garlic sauce, fresh cilantro, and lime juice.

08 Leftovers will keep covered in the refrigerator for 2-3 days, though best when fresh. Reheat in a 350 degree F oven until warmed through. See notes for freezing instructions.

Notes

*Cook quinoa in vegetable broth for extra flavor.

*To freeze, arrange the uncooked meatballs on a parchment-lined baking sheet and freeze until firm. Transfer to a freezer-safe container or bag and freeze for up to 1 month. To cook, place on a foil-lined baking sheet and spritz with oil to encourage browning. Bake for 20-30 minutes in a 350 degree F (176 degree C) oven, or until warmed through, gently tossing/flipping at the halfway point to ensure even cooking.

Hearty Cocoa Black Bean Burgers

This may just be my favorite veggie burger yet! I had long wondered if cocoa powder would work well in a smoky black bean burger, and I was seriously right in my suspicions. This burger is easy to make; loaded with healthy fats, protein, and fiber; and packed with diverse flavors thanks to a sultry blend of spices. Serve this to vegans and meat-eaters alike to satisfy that all-American burger craving.

SERVES 4 GENEROUSLY

PREP TIME 15 MIN. | COOK TIME 25 MIN. | TOTAL TIME 40 MIN.

1 cup (120g) raw walnuts

2-3 Tbsp (30-45ml) grape seed oil or avocado oil

½ medium white onion (~55g), finely diced

3 cloves garlic (1½ Tbsp or 9g), minced

Pinch each of salt and pepper, plus more to taste

1 Tbsp (8g) chili powder (reduce amount for less heat)

1 Tbsp (8g) ground cumin

3 Tbsp (18g) unsweetened cocoa powder (see note)

1 Tbsp (12g) coconut sugar (optional)

1 15-ounce (425g) can black beans, well rinsed, drained, and patted dry (see note)

1 cup (185g) cooked quinoa (see note)

01 Preheat the oven to 350 degrees F (176 degrees C). Arrange the walnuts on a rimmed baking sheet. Toast for 10 minutes, or until fragrant and light golden brown.

02 In the meantime, heat a large skillet over medium heat. Once hot, add 1 Tbsp (15ml) grape seed oil, onion, and garlic. Season with salt and pepper and sauté for 4-5 minutes, or until the onion is fragrant and translucent. Remove from heat and set aside.

03 Let the walnuts cool slightly, then add to the bowl of a food processor or blender. Add the chili powder, cumin, cocoa powder, a pinch each of salt and pepper, and coconut sugar (optional). Blend well. Set aside.

04 Add the drained black beans to a large bowl. Mash well with a fork, leaving only a few beans whole.

05 Add the quinoa, nut-spice mixture, garlic, and onion and mix to combine. The mixture should have a moldable dough texture. If dry, add extra 1-2 Tbsp (15-30ml) oil or a bit of water. If wet, add more walnut meal (or bread crumbs). Taste and adjust the seasonings as needed.

continued

06 Divide into 4 even patties. To help form, line a ½-cup measuring cup with plastic wrap and scoop out ½ cup (~150g) amounts. Press to pack, then lift out and slightly flatten with your hands so they are not as tall.

07 Heat the same skillet used earlier over medium heat. Once hot, add enough grape seed oil to form a thin layer on the bottom of the hot skillet (~2 Tbsp or 30ml).

08 Carefully add the burgers. Brown for 3-5 minutes on each side, flipping gently and reducing the heat if the burgers get too brown.

09 The burgers can either be served as is, or they can be popped on a baking sheet and baked in a 375 degree F (190 degree C) oven for an additional 10-20 minutes to dry/crisp them up a bit. But they are great as is! The longer they are baked, the drier/firmer they will become.

10 Cool for 2-3 minutes before serving (they will firm up as they cool).

11 Serve on toasted hamburger buns (gluten-free when necessary) with desired toppings. Leftovers will keep in the refrigerator for 2-3 days. See notes for freezing instructions.

Notes

*Total time does not include cooking quinoa.

*The cocoa is not an intense flavor, but can be reduced to play a smaller role in the burger. For a less prominent cocoa flavor, reduce the cocoa powder by 1 Tbsp (6g).

*If black beans are unsalted, add ¼ tsp extra salt to the burger mixture.

*For a simple burger sauce, mix 2 parts vegan mayonnaise and 1 part ketchup.

*To freeze, brown the burgers on either side as instructed. Then cool completely and freeze on a parchment-lined baking sheet for 4-6 hours, or until firm. Transfer to a freezer-safe bag or container. Freeze for up to 1 month. Reheat in a 375 degree F (190 degree C) oven on a parchment-lined baking sheet for 20-30 minutes, or until warmed through.

Thai Peanut Burgers

These veggie burgers are an infusion of some of my favorite Thai flavors. The chickpea base is incredibly hearty, peanut butter and soy sauce add loads of flavor, and chili garlic sauce ties everything together with a little heat. Serve with Peanut Sauce (page 10) and fresh carrots for extra sweetness and crunch.

SERVES 4 (YIELDS 8 PATTIES)

| PREP TIME 25 MIN. | COOK TIME 45 MIN. | TOTAL TIME 1 HR. 10 MIN. |

1 15-ounce (425g) can chickpeas, thoroughly rinsed, drained, and patted dry

½ cup (92g) cooked white quinoa

⅔ cup (67g) green onion, diced, plus more for serving

¼ cup (64g) salted creamy peanut butter

½ cup (70g) roasted salted or lightly salted peanuts, ground/crushed

2-3 Tbsp (30-45ml) tamari or soy sauce (if gluten-free, use tamari)

2-3 tsp chili garlic sauce

2 Tbsp (27g) organic brown sugar, packed (or substitute coconut sugar)

Pinch of sea salt

FOR SERVING (optional)
Hamburger buns

Chili garlic sauce and/or Peanut Sauce (page 10)

Green onion, diced

Carrots, thinly sliced

Red onion, sliced

Fresh cilantro

01 Preheat the oven to 375 degrees F (190 degrees C) and lightly grease a baking sheet.

02 In a large bowl, coarsely mash the chickpeas with a fork, leaving a few beans whole for texture.

03 Add the quinoa, green onion, peanut butter, crushed peanuts, tamari, chili garlic sauce, brown sugar, and a pinch of sea salt.

04 Stir to combine and adjust the seasonings as needed, adding more tamari or salt for saltiness, chili garlic sauce for spice, and brown sugar for sweetness. If the mixture is too wet to form into patties, add more ground peanuts.

05 To form patties, line a ¼-cup measuring cup with plastic wrap. Scoop in mixture and pack with hands, then fold over the edges of the plastic wrap to form a tight burger. Use the wrap to lift the burger out of the measuring cup. Place on a baking sheet. (Alternatively, use your hands to form patties.) Press down very slightly so the burger is not as tall. Repeat until all of the burgers are formed.

06 Bake for 20 minutes, carefully flip, then bake 15-20 minutes more. The longer they are baked, the crispier they will become.

07 Serve on hamburger buns (gluten-free when necessary) or lettuce wraps with desired toppings. Double stack the patties for a heartier burger.

08 Leftovers keep covered in the refrigerator for 2-3 days, though best when fresh. See notes for freezing instructions.

Notes

*Total time does not include cooking quinoa.

*To freeze, partially bake burgers for 20 minutes and let cool completely. Arrange on a baking sheet and freeze until firm. Transfer to a freezer-safe bag or container, inserting parchment paper between the patties to prevent sticking, and freeze for up to 1 month. To reheat, bake in a 350 degree F (176 degree C) oven for 20-30 minutes, or until warmed through.

Spicy BBQ Jackfruit Sandwiches with Grilled Pineapple

After having such success with my first BBQ Jackfruit Sandwich on the blog, I didn't want the fun to stop. This version has a slightly spicier flavor that is perfectly offset by grilled pineapple. It's smoky, spicy, sweet, and everything I am looking for in a pulled jackfruit sandwich.

SERVES 4

PREP TIME 5 MIN. | **COOK TIME 25 MIN.** | **TOTAL TIME 30 MIN.**

2 20-ounce (565g) cans young green jackfruit in water or brine

2 Tbsp (30ml) grape seed oil or avocado oil

¼ white or yellow onion (27g), diced

¾ cup (190g) BBQ sauce (page 12), plus more for topping (spicy is best)

4 pineapple rings sliced ¼ inch thick (cored)

4 vegan hamburger buns, toasted or grilled

½ medium red onion (55g), sliced (optional)

Green onion, diced (optional)

BBQ SPICE BLEND
¼ cup (55g) organic brown sugar (or substitute organic muscovado sugar or coconut sugar)

2 tsp garlic powder

1½ tsp smoked paprika

1 tsp ground cumin

1 tsp sea salt

continued

01 If the jackfruit is packed in water, drain, thoroughly dry, and move on to step 02. If the jackfruit is in brine, give it a thorough rinse to draw out some of the brine flavor. Then dry thoroughly in a clean towel.

02 To prune the jackfruit, think of it like a pineapple. The goal is to remove the "core" or hard, dense portions. Also, remove any other parts that don't look appetizing. You can get as picky as you want, but I like to remove any portions that have strange texture, such as the little bulb-like pieces.

03 Place the pruned jackfruit in a small bowl and use a fork to string/pull it apart. Set aside.

04 Mix the BBQ spice blend in a separate bowl. Add the brown sugar, garlic powder, paprika, cumin, salt, pepper, chili powder, and cayenne (optional). Then add to jackfruit and toss thoroughly to combine. In the meantime, heat a large skillet over medium heat.

05 Once the skillet is hot, add the grape seed oil and onion and sauté for 4-5 minutes or until slightly translucent. Add the jackfruit and sauté for 5 minutes to get a good sear on the edges.

continued

1 tsp black pepper

1 tsp chili powder

¼ tsp cayenne pepper
(optional)

06 Add the BBQ sauce and enough water to thin the mixture into a sauce (about ¼ cup or 60ml, depending on the thickness of the BBQ sauce).

07 Reduce the heat to low and simmer for 15-20 minutes, stirring occasionally, until the flavor has permeated the jackfruit. Add more BBQ sauce and/or water as needed.

08 In the meantime, grill or sauté the pineapple until slightly caramelized. If using a grill, rub the pineapple in oil, then grill for 1-3 minutes on each side, or until prominent grill marks appear. If using a skillet, heat over medium heat and, once hot, add the pineapple and a bit of oil. Cook on either side for 2-3 minutes, or until golden brown and caramelized. Set aside.

09 To toast the buns, either a grill or skillet can be used, or they can be placed cut-side up on a baking sheet and broiled on low for 3-4 minutes. Watch closely as to not let them burn.

10 To serve, add the grilled pineapple to toasted buns. Top with BBQ jackfruit. Serve with additional sauce and any desired vegetables (such as sliced red onion and green onion).

11 Store leftover jackfruit covered in the refrigerator for up to 4 days.

Pizza Burgers

Pizza may seem like an unlikely flavor application for a veggie burger, but it's one of the best I've tried! Chickpeas create a hearty, neutral base, while garlic and Italian seasonings impart big flavor. Serve this on a ciabatta bun with pizza sauce for a delicious pizza–inspired sandwich.

SERVES 4

PREP TIME 10 MIN. | **COOK TIME 20 MIN.** | **TOTAL TIME 30 MIN.**

2 shallots
(4 Tbsp or 40g), minced

3 cloves garlic
(1½ Tbsp or 9g), minced

4 Tbsp (60ml) olive oil
or grape seed oil, plus
more as needed

1 15-ounce (425g) can
chickpeas, rinsed and
drained

¼ cup (20g) Vegan
Parmesan (page 7), plus
more for serving

2 tsp Italian seasonings
(or 1 tsp each dried
basil and oregano)

¼ cup (15g) fresh
parsley, finely chopped

1 cup (74g) vegan-
friendly bread crumbs,
plus more for coating

3 Tbsp (47g) marinara
sauce (or pizza sauce),
plus more for topping
(see note)

¼ tsp each sea salt and
black pepper

FOR SERVING
1 cup (250g) marinara
or pizza sauce (see note)

4 ciabatta buns, toasted

Fresh parsley

Red onion

01 Heat a large skillet over medium heat. Once hot, sauté shallots and garlic in 1 Tbsp (15ml) olive oil until soft and translucent, 3-4 minutes, stirring frequently.

02 Add the cooked garlic and shallot directly to a medium bowl. Add the chickpeas and use a fork or pastry cutter to mash/mix. The mixture should be dough-like with only a few whole beans remaining.

03 Add 2 Tbsp (30ml) olive oil, the Vegan Parmesan, Italian seasonings parsley, bread crumbs, marinara, salt, and pepper. Stir to combine. A moldable "dough" should form. Add more olive oil if it's too dry, or more bread crumbs or Vegan Parmesan if too wet. Taste and adjust the seasonings as needed.

04 Heat the same skillet used earlier over medium heat.

05 Divide the mixture into 4 even patties. To help form them, line a ½-cup measuring cup with plastic wrap and scoop out ½ cup amounts. Press to pack, then lift them out and slightly flatten them with your hands. Alternatively, form into 1-inch-thick patties with your hands.

06 Gently coat the burgers with additional bread crumbs and Vegan Parmesan cheese on both sides for more flavor and texture (optional). Handle gently as they can be fragile.

continued

07 Add enough oil to form a thin layer on the bottom of hot skillet (~1 Tbsp or 30ml), then add the coated burgers. Brown for about 5 minutes on each side, reducing the heat if the burgers get too brown.

08 Serve the burgers as is, or pop them on a baking sheet and bake in a 375 degree F (190 degree C) oven for an additional 10-20 minutes to dry/crisp them up.

09 In the meantime, warm 1 cup (250g) marinara sauce, toast the ciabatta buns, and prep the parsley and onion.

10 To serve, lay down parsley on the bottom half of a bun, top with a burger, onion, marinara sauce, and additional Vegan Parmesan.

11 Leftover burgers will keep in the refrigerator for 3-4 days, though best when fresh. Reheat in a 350 degree F oven for 20 minutes, or until warmed through.

Note

*To make your own pizza sauce, add 1 cup (245g) tomato sauce to a small saucepan over medium heat. Season with 1 tsp each dried oregano, dried basil, dried garlic, sweetener of your choice, and a healthy pinch each of salt and pepper. Whisk to combine. Taste and adjust the seasonings as needed. Serve warm.

Smoky BBQ Veggie Burgers

Barbecue sauce is a top contender for my favorite condiment of all time. It's no wonder I figured out a way to infuse its flavor into a veggie burger. These quinoa and chickpea-based patties are hearty, loaded with smoky flavor, and come together in just 30 minutes. Serve on a bun with extra BBQ sauce, or alongside classic sides like baked beans and grilled corn for a flavorful, plant-based entrée.

SERVES 4

PREP TIME 10 MIN.	COOK TIME 20 MIN.	TOTAL TIME 30 MIN.

1 15-ounce (425g) can chickpeas, rinsed and drained

¾ cup (138g) cooked quinoa (see note)

½-¾ cup (20-30g) bread crumbs (see note)

1 tsp garlic powder, plus more to taste

1 tsp smoked paprika, plus more to taste

1 tsp ground cumin, plus more to taste

1¾ tsp sea salt, plus more to taste

1 tsp chili powder, plus more to taste

Pinch of cayenne pepper (optional)

1 Tbsp (12g) coconut sugar (or substitute organic brown sugar), plus more to taste

2-3 Tbsp (32-48g) BBQ sauce (page 12)

continued

01 Add the chickpeas to a medium bowl and mash with a pastry cutter or fork. Leave just a few beans whole for texture. Add the cooked quinoa, bread crumbs, garlic powder, paprika, cumin, salt, chili powder, cayenne (optional), coconut sugar, and 2 Tbsp (32g) BBQ sauce.

02 Stir/mash to combine with a wooden spoon. If the mixture appears too wet, add more bread crumbs. If mixture appears too dry (not moldable), add more BBQ sauce or a bit of grape seed oil. Taste and adjust the seasonings as needed, adding more salt, sugar for sweetness, or spices for depth of flavor.

03 Heat a large skillet over medium heat and form patties. For 4 large burgers, line a ½-cup measuring cup with plastic wrap and fill with the mixture. Press down firmly. Lift out and slightly flatten so the patty is not as tall. Transfer to a clean plate. Repeat until all 4 burgers are formed. For 6 burgers, use a ⅓-cup measuring cup.

04 Once the skillet is hot, add enough grape seed oil to coat the bottom generously (~2 Tbsp or 30ml). Sprinkle the tops of the burgers with a bit more salt and chili powder.

continued

2 Tbsp (30ml) grape seed
oil or avocado oil, plus
more to needed

FOR SERVING
Buns or lettuce wraps

Lettuce, onion, and/or
slaw

BBQ sauce

05 Gently place the seasoned side down.
Cook for 3-4 minutes, or until golden
brown. Season the top sides with a bit
more salt and chili powder, then gently
flip and cook for 3-4 minutes on the other
side. Reduce the heat if browning too
quickly.

06 The burgers can be served as is, or,
for firmer texture, continue cooking
on a baking sheet in a 350 degree F
oven (176 degrees C) for 15-30 minutes.
The longer the burgers are baked, the
firmer and crispier they will get. This
step is totally optional and depends on
preference.

07 Serve the burgers on lightly toasted
buns with your desired toppings.

08 Best when fresh, though leftovers keep
in the refrigerator for up to 3 days.
Freeze leftovers for up to 3-4 weeks.
Reheat in a 350 degree F oven for best
results.

Notes

*Total time does not include cooking the quinoa.

*Cook the quinoa in vegetable broth for extra
flavor.

*If you do not have bread crumbs, you can grind
day-old bread or 2-3 of your hamburger buns in
the bowl of a food processor or blender until a
crumbly meal is achieved.

Deep-Dish Pizza with Tofu Ricotta

Before going dairy-free, I made a deep-dish pizza for the blog that has since become one of our most popular recipes. I wanted to make a vegan version for the cookbook, which is possible with Vegan Parmesan (page 7) and tofu ricotta. The crust gets golden and crispy in a cast-iron skillet, tomato sauce adds a rich, sweet flavor, and the combination of vegan cheeses sends this dish over the top. Pizza night just got an upgrade.

SERVES 4

PREP TIME 15 MIN. | **COOK TIME 30 MIN.** | **TOTAL TIME 45 MIN.**

1½ Tbsp (22ml) olive oil, plus more to coat bottom of the skillet

1 store-bought vegan pizza dough (~450g)

¾ cup (183g) pizza sauce (see note)

6 ounces (170g) extra-firm tofu, drained and pressed for 10 minutes in a clean towel

1½ lemons, juiced (~3 Tbsp or 45ml), plus more to taste

2 Tbsp (6g) nutritional yeast, plus more to taste

½ cup loosely packed (30g) fresh basil, chopped (or substitute 1 Tbsp or 3g dried)

1½ tsp dried oregano

Scant ½ tsp each sea salt and black pepper, plus more to taste

6 Tbsp (30g) Vegan Parmesan (page 7)

01 Preheat the oven to 450 degrees F (232 degrees C). Lightly coat a 12-inch cast-iron skillet with enough olive oil to just coat the bottom.

02 Measure out the pizza sauce (or prepare, if making from scratch), and set out pizza dough to soften.

03 To prepare the tofu ricotta, add the tofu, lemon juice, nutritional yeast, olive oil, basil, oregano, salt, pepper, and 2 Tbsp (10g) Vegan Parmesan to the bowl of a food processor or blender.

04 Pulse to combine, scraping down the sides as needed. The mixture should be semipuréed, with bits of basil still intact. Taste and adjust the seasonings as needed, adding more salt and pepper for flavor, nutritional yeast for cheesiness, and lemon juice for brightness. Put in the refrigerator to chill while preparing the remaining ingredients.

05 Press the pizza dough down into the prepared pan. Push it up around the sides about 1½ inches and sprinkle in 2 Tbsp (10g) Vegan Parmesan.

06 Add the pizza sauce, then dot on the tofu ricotta in 1 Tbsp (15g) amounts.

continued

There will likely be leftover ricotta filling, which can be used for future pizzas or other Italian dishes, such as my Classic Vegan Lasagna (page 207). Leftovers keep for 7-10 days in the refrigerator.

07 Top with the remaining 2 Tbsp (10g) Vegan Parmesan and bake on the center rack for 25-30 minutes, or until the crust is golden brown and the sauce is bubbly.

08 Let rest for 5 minutes before serving. Leftovers will keep covered in the refrigerator for 1-2 days, though best when fresh. Reheat leftovers on a baking sheet in a 350 degree F oven until hot, 10-15 minutes.

Note

*Pizza sauce recipe: ¾ cup (183g) tomato sauce plus 1 tsp each dried basil, dried oregano, garlic powder, and organic cane sugar or maple syrup. Add sea salt to taste and whisk. You can also substitute one 6-ounce (170g) can tomato paste and 1 cup (240ml) water for the tomato sauce.

Angel Hair Pasta with Harissa Romesco

This has to be one of my absolute favorite pastas to date! The romesco sauce packs a serious punch with roasted almonds, red bell peppers, and tomato. Garlic, red wine vinegar, and harissa paste add depth of flavor. Keep it gluten-free by using gluten-free noodles. Cheers to pasta night!

SERVES 4 | **PREP TIME 10 MIN.** | **COOK TIME 20 MIN.** | **TOTAL TIME 30 MIN.**

10 ounces (283g) angel hair or linguini pasta (see note)

1 ripe tomato (123g)

2 red bell peppers (238g)

½ cup (56g) raw almonds

4 cloves garlic (12g), skin on

1 Tbsp (15ml) grape seed oil or avocado oil

¼ cup (60ml) olive oil

1-2 Tbsp (15-30ml) red wine vinegar (reduce for less acidity)

¼ tsp smoked paprika

½ tsp sea salt

1-2 Tbsp (15-30ml) maple syrup

1-2 tsp harissa paste or ¼ tsp red pepper flake

FOR SERVING (optional)
2-3 Tbsp (10-15g) Vegan Parmesan (page 7)

Fresh parsley or basil, chopped

01 Preheat the oven to 425 degrees F (218 degrees C).

02 In the meantime, cook the pasta according to the package instructions, drain, and set aside. Cover the pasta with a towel to keep warm.

03 Arrange tomato and bell peppers, still whole with stems, on one end of a rimmed baking sheet. On the other end of the baking sheet, arrange the almonds and garlic (still in skin). Lightly drizzle the garlic with the grape seed oil.

04 Place the baking sheet in the oven and roast the almonds for 6-7 minutes, then remove from pan and set aside. Bake garlic for another 5-8 minutes, then remove and set aside.

05 Allow tomato and red pepper to roast until the skin is bubbled and mostly blackened, turning/flipping periodically to char all sides.

06 Once charred, wrap the roasted red peppers in foil to steam for 2-3 minutes, then peel away the skin, seeds, and core. Also, remove the core of the tomato and remove the skin from the garlic.

07 Add the peeled peppers, cored tomato, almonds, garlic, olive oil, vinegar, paprika, salt, maple syrup, and harissa to

continued

the bowl of a blender or food processor. Purée until smooth, scraping down the sides as needed. Taste and adjust the seasonings as desired, adding more harissa paste for heat, vinegar for acidity, or salt for balance.

08 Serve over pasta with Vegan Parmesan and any desired fresh herbs. Leftovers keep well, covered in the refrigerator, for 3-4 days, though best when fresh.

Note

*To keep this recipe gluten-free, use your favorite gluten-free pasta noodle, the thinner in shape and size the better.

Butternut Squash Garlic Mac 'n' Cheese

This recipe rocks my world! If you are a serious mac 'n' cheese fan, this is the recipe for you. Butternut squash adds a vibrant orange hue and a creamy base, while nutritional yeast packs in tons of cheesy flavor. It's also gluten-free when using gluten-free pasta, which I have found to be so rich in protein, this is easily a meal in itself!

SERVES 2 AS ENTRÉE, 4 AS SIDE

PREP TIME 10 MIN. | **COOK TIME 20 MIN.** | **TOTAL TIME 30 MIN.**

Sea salt, to taste

8 ounces (227g) gluten-free quinoa fusilli pasta (or whole wheat pasta)

2 cups (280g) cubed butternut squash (see note)

2 Tbsp (30ml) grape seed oil or avocado oil

Black pepper, to taste

4 cloves garlic (2 Tbsp or 12g), minced

¾ cup (180ml) unsweetened plain almond milk or DIY Almond Milk (page 6)

3 Tbsp (45ml) vegetable broth

3-4 Tbsp (9-12g) nutritional yeast, plus more to taste

¼ tsp chili garlic sauce or hot sauce (optional)

FOR SERVING (*optional*)
Vegan Parmesan (page 7)

Fresh parsley, minced

Red pepper flakes

01 Preheat the oven to 400 degrees F (204 degrees C). Bring a large pot of water to a boil over high heat and salt liberally. Add the pasta and cook according to the package instructions, drain, and set aside. Cover with a towel to keep warm.

02 While the pasta is cooking, add the butternut squash to foil-lined rimmed baking sheet. Drizzle with 1 Tbsp (15ml) grape seed oil and sprinkle with a healthy pinch each of salt and pepper. Toss to coat.

03 Bake for 12-14 minutes, or until fork tender. Remove from the oven and add to the bowl of a high-speed blender or food processor. Set aside.

04 Heat the same saucepan used earlier to cook the pasta over medium heat. Once hot, add the remaining 1 Tbsp (15ml) of grape seed oil and the garlic. Sauté for 2 minutes or until fragrant. Stir frequently.

05 Add the garlic to the blender or processor with the butternut squash. Add another healthy pinch of salt and pepper, almond milk, broth, and nutritional yeast. Blend until creamy and smooth. The sauce should be thick but pourable, so add more broth or almond milk to thin if necessary. Taste and adjust the flavor as needed, adding more nutritional yeast for cheesiness, or a bit of chili garlic sauce or hot sauce for heat (optional).

continued

06 Add the mixture back to the saucepan. Bring to a low simmer over medium-low heat. Cook to heat/thicken for 5 minutes, stirring frequently.

07 Add the cooked, drained pasta to the sauce and toss to coat. Serve immediately with Vegan Parmesan, red pepper flakes, and fresh parsley (optional).

08 Leftovers will keep covered in the refrigerator for 2-3 days, though best when fresh.

Note

*The best way to cube butternut squash is to start with a large, very sharp knife, cutting off the top and bottom portions. Then cut in half where the small, cylinder shape and round, bulb shape meet. Use a knife to carefully remove the skin. Then remove any seeds with a spoon. Cut into small cubes and proceed with the recipe as directed.

Peanut Butter Pad Thai

I have been making Pad Thai for dinner almost weekly for years now. There is something incredibly addictive about the sticky rice noodles combined with the tangy-sweet sauce. This version infuses peanut butter into the mix for a creamy, savory finish. Crispy baked tofu provides extra protein and texture, and fresh carrots and green onion add a colorful finishing touch.

SERVES 2 AS ENTRÉE, 4 AS SIDE

PREP TIME 10 MIN. | **COOK TIME 40 MIN.** | **TOTAL TIME 50 MIN.**

12 ounces (340g) extra-firm tofu

6 ounces (170g) thin rice noodles

3 cloves garlic (1½ Tbsp or 9g), minced

1 large bundle (6 ounces or 170g) green onion, finely chopped

2 whole carrots (122g), ribboned with a vegetable peeler or thinly diced

SAUCE
2 Tbsp (32g) salted creamy peanut butter

3 Tbsp (45g) tamarind concentrate or paste (see note)

4½ Tbsp (68ml) tamari or soy sauce (if gluten-free, use tamari)

3-4 Tbsp (45-60ml) maple syrup (or substitute coconut sugar)

1½ tsp chili garlic sauce, plus more for serving

FOR SERVING (optional)
Peanut Sauce (page 10)

Chili garlic sauce

Freshly squeezed lime juice

01 Preheat the oven to 400 degrees F (204 degrees C) and line a rimmed baking sheet with parchment paper.

02 Wrap the tofu in a clean, absorbent towel and set something heavy on top, such as a cast-iron skillet, to aid in draining the moisture.

03 Once the oven is hot, cube the tofu into bite-size pieces and arrange on the prepared baking sheet. Bake for 28-30 minutes. Depending on the firmness of the tofu, the cooking times will vary. The longer it bakes, the firmer and chewier it gets, which I prefer. Check for doneness at the 28-minute mark and bake longer if desired.

04 In the meantime, make the sauce. To a small skillet add the peanut butter, tamarind concentrate, 3 Tbsp (45ml) tamari, 3 Tbsp (45ml) maple syrup, and 1 tsp chili garlic sauce. Heat over medium heat. When the sauce begins bubbling, stir and reduce the heat to low. Simmer for 5 minutes, then turn off heat and let rest. Taste and adjust the flavor as needed, adding more chili garlic sauce for heat, maple syrup for sweetness, or tamari for saltiness. The flavor should be sour-sweet.

continued

05 When the tofu is almost done baking, cook the rice noodles according to the package instructions. Then drain and set aside.

06 Heat a large skillet over medium heat. Once hot, add the baked tofu, 1 Tbsp (15ml) pad Thai sauce, 1 Tbsp (15ml) tamari, and the remaining ½ tsp chili garlic sauce. Stir frequently and cook until brown on all sides, about 4 minutes. Remove from the pan and set aside.

07 To the same skillet, add the garlic and green onion (reserving a small amount for garnish), and ½ Tbsp (8ml) more tamari. Sauté for 2-3 minutes, stirring frequently. Add the cooked noodles and the remaining Pad Thai sauce and toss with tongs to coat. Raise the heat to medium-high and cook for 2-3 minutes, stirring frequently. Add the tofu during the last minute of cooking to warm through.

08 Remove from the heat and serve with the carrots, the reserved green onions, Peanut Sauce (optional), and additional chili garlic sauce.

09 Leftovers keep covered in the refrigerator for 2-3 days, though best when fresh.

Note

*Tamarind concentrate can be found online and in Asian grocery stores. It may seem like a rare ingredient, but I always have some on hand for cooking Asian dishes, especially pad Thai.

Sweet Potato Sage Raviolis

Yes, making raviolis at home is possible and surprisingly easy! This sweet potato version is more of a time commitment than my other recipes, but the payoff is totally worth it. Plus, if you make the whole batch, you can freeze leftovers for quick, premade meals. The filling is sweet, the walnuts add a crunchy, nutty bite, and the sage makes this dish feel like autumn.

SERVES 6 (YIELDS ~50 RAVIOLIS)

PREP TIME 40 MIN. | **COOK TIME 1 HR. 30 MIN.** | **TOTAL TIME 2 HR. 10 MIN.**

FILLING
2 large organic sweet potatoes (~1 lb or 453g)

¼ tsp sea salt

2 Tbsp (24g) coconut sugar or organic cane sugar

1 tsp ground cinnamon

PASTA
2 cups (336g) semolina flour, plus more for rolling

½ cup (68g) unbleached all-purpose flour

¾-1 cup (180-240ml) room-temperature water

1 tsp olive oil

FOR SERVING
½ cup (60g) raw walnuts, coarsely chopped

¼ cup (8g) fresh sage, coarsely chopped

2-3 Tbsp (30-45ml) olive oil

¼ cup (20g) Vegan Parmesan (page 7)

01 Preheat the oven to 400 degrees F (204 degrees C). Bake the whole sweet potatoes directly on the oven rack for 1 hour to 1 hour 15 minutes, depending on their size. They're done when tender to the touch and a knife slides in and out with ease.

02 Let the potatoes cool briefly, then remove the skins, add to a medium bowl, and mash. Season with the salt, coconut sugar, and cinnamon. Stir, then set aside to cool in the refrigerator.

03 Next, prepare the pasta. Add the semolina and all-purpose flour to a large bowl and whisk. In a separate bowl, mix water with the olive oil. Add to the dry ingredients 1 Tbsp at a time, mixing with a wooden spoon to combine. Stop adding water when a loose dough has formed.

04 Transfer the pasta dough to a surface dusted with semolina. Knead for 3 minutes or until elastic and slightly sticky. Wrap in plastic wrap and let rest for 20-30 minutes or in refrigerator for up to 2 days. (Alternatively, store in freezer in freezer-safe container for up to 2 weeks.)

05 Unwrap the pasta dough and divide into two even pieces. Set aside one half, and place the other half on a clean surface liberally dusted with semolina.

continued

06 Use a rolling pin to roll the pasta dough into a large square almost as thin as paper. Add more semolina to the surface and top of the pasta dough as you go, to prevent sticking. Use a pizza cutter or knife to cut the pasta dough into 6 even strips about 1½ inches wide.

07 Use a teaspoon or similar-size spoon to scoop small amounts of chilled sweet potato filling (~7g). Scoop onto 3 of the 6 pasta strips, leaving ½ inch of space between the dollops and the edge to allow room to close the raviolis.

08 Wet your finger or a brush and run it along the edges of the pasta to help the sheets stick together. Then, one at a time, carefully pick up a strip of bare pasta, flip it over, and gently lay it down on top of an adjacent strip with filling. Use your finger to gently press down in between the spaces of the filling to aid in the cutting process.

09 Use a pizza cutter or knife (or ravioli stamper) to cut the raviolis into squares. Then use a fork to crimp the edges, gently stretching the pasta down over the filling to meet the edges and prevent spillover as needed. Trim any edges using the pizza cutter or knife as needed, and transfer the ravioli to a parchment-lined baking sheet as you go.

10 Repeat until all of the raviolis are filled (re-forming any leftover scraps and rolling them out again to repeat the process). You should have about 50 total.

11 Allow the raviolis to dry on the baking sheets for 10-15 minutes to prevent sticking. (Alternatively, place them in the freezer to cook later. Transfer baking sheets to the freezer to let the raviolis freeze entirely. Once frozen, store in a freezer-safe container for later use.)

12 When ready to cook, bring a large pot of water to a boil. Salt well. Add 9 or 10 raviolis at a time. Cook for 3-4 minutes if fresh, and 5-6 minutes if frozen. Then use a slotted spoon to scoop out the raviolis. Set aside. Continue until all the raviolis are boiled.

13 After raviolis are done cooking, place a large skillet over medium heat and prep the walnuts and sage.

14 Add 1 Tbsp (15ml) olive oil to the hot skillet, then add 1 Tbsp each walnuts and sage, reserving the rest for other batches. Stir and sauté for 1 minute, then add only as many raviolis as will fit comfortably in the pan. Cook on both sides for 1-2 minutes. The goal is a quick sear. Flip carefully and add more oil as needed to prevent sticking.

15 Transfer the seared raviolis to a serving platter (which can be kept warm in a 200 degree F oven). Continue the cooking process (adding oil, then walnuts and sage, then ravioli) until all of the raviolis are cooked.

16 Serve with Vegan Parmesan. Store leftovers covered in the refrigerator for up to 2 days, though best when fresh.

17 Raw (uncooked) raviolis will keep in the refrigerator for 1-2 days, and in the freezer up to 1 month.

Herb-Marinated Tofu

If you are looking to take your tofu to the next level, try this simple marinade. It infuses a beautiful lemon–herb flavor into any dish you add it to. Once marinated, this tofu makes a delicious base for tofu scrambles, bruschetta, and more!

SERVES 7

PREP TIME 3 HRS. 10 MIN. | **TOTAL TIME 3 HRS. 10 MIN.**

1 14-ounce (397g) block extra-firm tofu, patted dry (see note)

2½ cups (600ml) filtered water

3 tsp sea salt

MARINADE
½ tsp sea salt

Pinch of black pepper

¼ cup (60ml) freshly squeezed lemon juice

2 cloves garlic (1 Tbsp or 6g), minced

1 Tbsp (15ml) maple syrup (optional)

½ cup (30g) parsley

½ cup (30g) basil

½ cup (120ml) olive oil

01 Wrap/press the tofu in a clean towel to dry slightly, then cut into 1-inch cubes. Place in an 8 x 8-inch or similar size shallow dish.

02 Bring the water and salt to a boil to make a brine, then pour over the tofu. Let soak for 1 hour (up to 3), uncovered, at room temperature.

03 In the meantime, prepare the marinade in the bowl of a food processor or blender by blending/pulsing all of the ingredients together until well incorporated. Alternatively, mince herbs/garlic and whisk ingredients together in a large bowl. Set aside.

04 Drain the brine from the tofu, then pat dry in a clean towel. Place the tofu in a dry, shallow dish and add the marinade. Toss to coat. Cover and let marinate for at least 2 hours, preferably overnight, in the refrigerator.

05 Serve the marinated tofu chilled or at room temperature in salads. This also makes an excellent base for tofu scrambles. It will keep covered in the refrigerator for up to 5 days.

Notes

*The quality of the tofu definitely stands out in this recipe, so be sure to buy the freshest, highest-quality tofu possible. If possible, look for a local vendor.

*You could also use this as a base for tofu ricotta in recipes like my Deep-Dish Pizza with Tofu Ricotta (page 187) and Classic Vegan Lasagna (page 207).

Simple Tomato + Lentil Ragu

This is weeknight spaghetti kicked up a notch thanks to lentils—a nutritional powerhouse. This ragu is hearty, simple to make, and loaded with fresh garlic and Italian flavors. Serve it atop gluten-free pasta with Vegan Parmesan and fresh basil for a flavor-packed, plant-based entrée.

SERVES 4

PREP TIME 10 MIN.	COOK TIME 50 MIN.	TOTAL TIME 60 MIN.

½ cup (96g) dry green lentils (well rinsed and drained)

1 cup (240ml) water (or substitute vegetable broth)

½ cup (64g) carrots, diced

½ yellow or white onion (55g), minced

4 cloves garlic (2 Tbsp or 12g), minced

1 Tbsp (15ml) olive oil, grape seed oil, or avocado oil

Pinch each of sea salt and black pepper

1 28-ounce (794g) can tomato sauce

2 tsp Italian seasoning (or 1 tsp each dried oregano and basil)

1-2 Tbsp (12-24g) coconut sugar (or substitute organic cane sugar or maple syrup)

¼ tsp red pepper flakes, for heat (optional)

01 Add the lentils and water (or broth for added flavor) to a small saucepan. Bring to a boil over high heat. Once boiling, reduce the heat to low, cover, and simmer until the lentils are cooked through and the liquid is absorbed, 35-40 minutes.

02 In the meantime, heat a large saucepan or cast-iron skillet over medium heat. Prep the carrots, onion, and garlic.

03 Once the saucepan is hot, add the olive oil, carrots, onion, and garlic. Season with a healthy pinch of each salt and pepper. Stir to coat and cover. Cook for 4 minutes, stirring occasionally.

04 Remove the cover and add tomato sauce, Italian seasoning, and coconut sugar (and red pepper flakes if desired), as well as another healthy pinch of salt and pepper. Stir, reduce the heat to low, and simmer for 10-15 minutes, stirring occasionally.

05 Transfer half of the sauce to the bowl of a food processor or high-speed blender and purée until creamy and smooth. For a chunky sauce, skip this step.

06 Add the sauce back to the saucepan. Bring to a simmer over medium-low heat. Taste and adjust the seasonings as needed, adding more herbs for depth, coconut sugar for sweetness, red pepper flakes for heat, or salt for balance.

continued

continued

FOR SERVING *(optional)*
Pasta (gluten-free when
necessary)

Fresh basil, chopped

Vegan Parmesan (page 7)

07 Add the cooked lentils and simmer for
5 minutes more, then serve. Alternatively,
the lentils can be kept separate and
served on top of the sauce.

08 This is the perfect hearty sauce for
weeknight pasta. Serve with gluten-free
pasta (quinoa and brown rice pasta being
my favorite), which often adds a little
more protein, basil, and Vegan Parmesan.

09 Store leftovers covered in the
refrigerator for up to 5 days, or in
the freezer for up to 1 month.

Classic
Vegan Lasagna

If I were to choose my last meal on earth, it would be lasagna. I love the layers of ricotta, pasta, and rich tomato sauce more than I can possibly explain. This is my vegan version, utilizing tofu ricotta for the filling, no-boil noodles, and store-bought tomato sauce to save on time. All in all, this recipe requires just a little over an hour to prepare and will leave you so satisfied, you'll not even miss the dairy.

SERVES 9

| PREP TIME 25 MIN. | COOK TIME 45 MIN. | TOTAL TIME 1 HR. 10 MIN. |

2 lemons, juiced
(~4-5 Tbsp or 60-75ml),
plus more to taste

12 ounces (340g) extra-firm tofu, drained and pressed dry in a clean towel for 10 minutes

3 Tbsp (12g) nutritional yeast, plus more to taste

½ cup (30g) fresh basil, finely chopped

1 Tbsp (3g) dried oregano

3-4 Tbsp (45-60ml) olive oil

~½ tsp each sea salt and black pepper, plus more to taste

¼ cup (20g) Vegan Parmesan (page 7), plus more for serving

26 ounces (737g) marinara sauce (see note)

8-10 no-boil lasagna noodles (more or less depending on the size of the dish; see note)

01 Preheat the oven to 375 degrees F (190 degrees C) and lightly grease an 8 × 8-inch (or similar size) baking dish.

02 Add the lemon juice, tofu, nutritional yeast, basil, oregano, olive oil, salt, pepper, and Vegan Parmesan to the bowl of a food processor or blender. Pulse to combine, scraping down the sides as needed. The mixture should be semi-puréed with bits of basil still intact.

03 Taste and adjust the seasonings as needed, adding more salt and pepper as desired, nutritional yeast for cheesiness, or lemon juice for acidity. Set aside.

04 Spread a thin layer of marinara sauce in the bottom of the prepared baking dish and top with a single layer of no-boil lasagna noodles.

05 Scoop on a generous amount (~⅓ cup or 75g) of tofu ricotta filling and spread it in an even layer. Top with a generous layer of marinara sauce.

06 Lay down lasagna noodles in the opposite direction of the first layer (to help stabilize the dish) and top with filling, sauce, and another layer of pasta in the opposite direction of the second layer. Repeat until all of the filling is used up.

continued

07 Make sure the top layer of pasta is topped with marinara and a sprinkle of Vegan Parmesan.

08 Cover with foil and bake for 30 minutes. Remove the foil and bake for another 10-15 minutes or until the sauce is bubbly and warm, and the pasta feels tender and cooked through.

09 Remove from the oven and let rest for 10-15 minutes before serving. Serve with additional Vegan Parmesan and fresh basil if desired.

10 Leftovers keep, covered, in the refrigerator for 2-3 days, though best when fresh.

Notes

*If you prefer to make your own marinara, use my Simple Tomato + Lentil Ragu on page 205 and leave out the lentils.

*If you cannot find no-boil noodles, boil the lasagna noodles, drain, and proceed through the recipe as instructed, but reduce the baking time by about 15 minutes. Alternatively, substitute thin slices of lightly roasted eggplant.

*To add more vegetables to this dish, add sautéed yellow or zucchini squash between each layer of tofu ricotta and sauce.

*To make a smaller lasagna for 2-4 people, halve the ingredients and prepare in a 9 x 5-inch loaf pan.

BLACKBERRY CUSTARD PIE, PAGE 225

Desserts

I'M A DESSERTS-LOVER AT HEART AND THIS COOKBOOK WOULDN'T BE COMPLETE without a few sweet endings.

In the following pages you'll find a smattering of seasonal dishes, fruit-heavy nibbles, and chocolaty things. Plus, I've included a few fall-inspired treats to get you through the holiday season.

It's all here and it's all delicious. Don't forget the coconut whipped cream topping!

*Requires an ice cream maker

Toasted Coconut Dark Chocolate Popcorn

If you have never popped your own popcorn, now is your chance! This simple dessert combines two of my favorite flavors: chocolate and toasted coconut. It's quick to make and is ideal for snacking or when you need a dessert that's quick and delicious.

SERVES 6	PREP TIME 5 MIN.	COOK TIME 15 MIN.	TOTAL TIME 20 MIN.

1 cup (80g) unsweetened coconut flakes

4 Tbsp (60ml) melted coconut oil

1 Tbsp (15ml) maple syrup or agave nectar

1 cup (120g) vegan dark chocolate, chopped

1½ cups (300g) unpopped popcorn kernels

Sea salt

01 Preheat the oven to 350 degrees F (176 degrees C). Add the coconut to a small bowl with 1 Tbsp (15ml) melted coconut oil and the maple syrup. Toss to coat. Spread on a baking sheet and bake for 3-5 minutes, watching closely, as it browns quickly. Remove from the oven and set aside.

02 Melt the chocolate over a double boiler or in your microwave in 30-second increments. Once completely melted, set aside.

03 Heat a large pot or saucepan over high heat and ready a large bowl for serving. Once the pot is hot, reduce the heat slightly to medium-high and add 1 Tbsp (15ml) coconut oil. Immediately add ½ cup (100g) popcorn kernels and a healthy pinch of salt. Shake the pan back and forth to coat.

04 Once the first couple of kernels start popping, cover with a lid and shake every 10 seconds to allow the unpopped kernels to settle to the bottom. Continue shaking every 10 seconds until the popping has mostly stopped, about 45 seconds. Transfer immediately to the large bowl and season with another pinch of salt. If the kernels are burnt, discard, reduce the heat, and try again.

05 Continue this process, adding 1 Tbsp (15 ml) coconut oil per ½ cup (100g) popcorn kernels, until all of the popcorn is popped.

06 Once the desired amount of popcorn is popped, top with the toasted coconut and drizzle with the melted dark chocolate. Serve immediately. Best when hot.

5-Ingredient Peppermint Patties

Cool and minty with an intensely dark chocolate coating, these plant-based beauties are insanely delicious. Serve as a refreshing after-dinner dessert or enjoy as a snack—either way you can't go wrong!

YIELDS 14 PATTIES

| PREP TIME 29 MIN. | COOK TIME 1 MIN. | TOTAL TIME 30 MIN. |

3 cups (240g) shredded unsweetened coconut

2 Tbsp (30ml) maple syrup

½-¾ tsp peppermint extract (for best quality, use food-grade peppermint oil)

2 tsp coconut oil

1 cup (120g) vegan dark chocolate, chopped

01 Add the shredded coconut to the bowl of a food processor or high-speed blender. Blend, scraping down the sides as needed, until a paste forms. The texture should feel like dough when squeezed between your fingers. It may be necessary to encourage it along by scraping down the sides as it's blending.

02 Add maple syrup, peppermint extract, and 1 tsp melted coconut oil. Mix again until incorporated. Again, look for a dough-like consistency. Scrape down the sides as needed. Scoop out the mixture and pack firmly using a tablespoon. Then roll between your palms to form a ball, and gently press down to form a disc. Use your fingers to gently pat them down so the patties are not too tall.

03 Place the patties on a parchment-lined baking sheet or plate, and continue until all of the coconut is used—the recipe should make about 14 patties. Place in the freezer to set for 10 minutes.

04 Melt the chocolate and remaining 1 tsp coconut oil over a double boiler or in your microwave in 30-second increments until melted.

05 Individually place a chilled patty on the prongs of a fork to dip into chocolate. Tap off any excess and set back on the parchment. Continue until all of the patties are coated.

06 Place in refrigerator or freezer to set for 8-10 minutes or until the chocolate is firm.

07 Peel the patties away from the parchment and transfer to a serving platter. Serve at room temperature or chilled. The patties will keep covered at room temperature for 3-4 days, or in the freezer (my preference) for up to 1 month. Best when fresh.

1-Bowl Jumbo Chocolate Chip Cookies

Sometimes you just need a chocolate chip cookie. With its perfectly soft center and crisp edges, this vegan version does not lack in flavor or texture. A sprinkle of sea salt adds a perfect savory-sweet finish.

12 LARGE COOKIES	PREP TIME 30 MIN.	COOK TIME 16 MIN.	TOTAL TIME 46 MIN.

1 stick (½ cup or 112g) vegan butter, softened (see note)

¼ cup (50g) organic cane sugar

½ cup (110g) organic brown sugar

1 tsp pure vanilla extract

3 Tbsp (37½g) pumpkin purée or unsweetened applesauce (see note)

1½ cups plus 2 Tbsp (221g) unbleached all-purpose flour

1½ tsp cornstarch or arrowroot starch

1 tsp baking powder

½ tsp baking soda

¼ tsp sea salt, plus more for the topping

½ cup (90g) vegan dark chocolate chips

01 Add the softened butter to large bowl and cream using a standing mixer for 1 minute.

02 Add the sugar, brown sugar, and vanilla. Beat for 1 minute more. Add the pumpkin and mix once more.

03 Set a sifter (see note) over something that will catch fallout (such as paper) and add the all-purpose flour, cornstarch, baking powder, baking soda, and salt. Use a spoon to gently stir the ingredients together, then sift over the wet ingredients.

04 Beat on medium speed until just incorporated, being careful not to overmix. Stir in chocolate chips, cover, and freeze the dough for 15 minutes, or refrigerate for 30 minutes (or chill overnight).

05 Preheat the oven to 350 degrees F (176 degrees C). Position a rack in the center of the oven.

06 Scoop out heaping 2½ Tbsp (~43g) amounts of dough, roll into balls, then flatten into discs. For smaller cookies, scoop out heaping 1 Tbsp (18g) amounts.

07 Top with a sprinkle of salt and place on a baking sheet 2 inches apart to allow for spreading.

continued

08 Bake on the center rack for 12-16 minutes (8-10 minutes for smaller cookies), or until very slightly golden brown on the edges. Remove from the oven and let rest on the baking sheet for 3 minutes, then transfer to a cooling rack to cool completely.

09 Store leftovers in a covered container for 3-4 days, though best when fresh. Freeze for longer storage.

Notes

*To speed the softening process, slice the vegan butter into ¼-inch pieces.

*If you do not have pumpkin purée, substitute a comparable amount of applesauce or 1 prepared Flax Egg (page 6).

*If you do not own a sifter, simply whisk together the dry ingredients in a separate bowl and add to the wet ingredients as instructed.

Dark Chocolate Almond Coconut Bites

These bites are one of my favorite desserts yet! Consider these my lazy-girl's take on classic Almond Joys. The base is a naturally sweetened, no-bake coconut cookie dunked in dark chocolate and topped with a roasted almond and more chocolate. Serve these delectable bites as a simple dessert, or enjoy throughout the week as a relatively guilt-free snack!

YIELDS 20 BITES

PREP TIME 25 MIN.	COOK TIME 1 MIN.	TOTAL TIME 26 MIN.

3 cups (240g) unsweetened shredded coconut

2 Tbsp (30ml) maple syrup

¼ tsp pure vanilla extract

20 roasted unsalted almonds or raw almonds (see note)

¾ cup (90g) vegan dark chocolate, chopped

OPTIONAL
Pinch of sea salt, for topping

01 Add the coconut to the bowl of a food processor or high-speed blender. Blend, scraping down the sides as needed, until a paste forms. The texture should feel like a dough when squeezed between your fingers. It may be necessary to encourage it along by scraping down the sides as it is blending.

02 Add the maple syrup and vanilla. Mix again until just incorporated.

03 Using a tablespoon, scoop out 1 Tbsp amounts and pack with your hands to achieve half-moon shapes. Then use a finger to scoop it out of the tablespoon. Re-form into a small disc if it loses shape.

04 Lay the bites down on a parchment-lined baking sheet. Continue until all of the coconut is used, about 20 bites.

05 Press one almond gently down into each of the bites, being careful not to create too much of a crack or seam. Set aside.

06 Melt the chocolate over a double boiler or in the microwave in 30-second increments. Then rest one coconut bite on a fork and hold it over the bowl. Use a spoon to drizzle chocolate over the top. Set back on the parchment paper and continue until all of the bites

continued

are coated. Sprinkle the tops with a bit of salt for flavor contrast (optional).

07 Pop the bites into the refrigerator or freezer to set for 8-10 minutes. Then pick up and, using a spoon, coat/paint the underside of the bites with the remaining melted chocolate.

08 Place back on the parchment paper and repeat until all of the bites are coated. Pop back in freezer to set for another 10 minutes.

09 Peel away from the parchment paper and transfer to a serving platter. Serve at room temperature or chilled. Leftovers will keep covered at room temperature for 3-4 days, or in the freezer for up to 1 month.

Note

*If the almonds are raw, roast them on a rimmed baking sheet in a 350 degree F (176 degree C) oven for 8-10 minutes, or until fragrant and slightly browned.

Chocolate-Dunked Peanut Butter Cookies

Peanut butter and chocolate were meant to be together, especially in cookie form. These salty-sweet gems are tender on the inside, crisp on the edges, and dipped in dark chocolate. What more could you ask for? Perhaps a glass of almond milk. Hello, dessert perfection!

YIELDS 20 COOKIES

| PREP TIME 55 MIN. | COOK TIME 15 MIN. | TOTAL TIME 1 HR. 10 MIN. |

1 stick (½ cup or 112g) vegan butter, softened (see note)

½ cup (128g) creamy salted peanut butter or almond butter

¼ cup (50g) organic cane sugar, plus more for topping

½ cup (110g) organic brown sugar, packed

1 tsp pure vanilla extract

2½ Tbsp (31g) pumpkin purée (see note)

1¼ cups (170g) unbleached all-purpose flour

¼ tsp sea salt, plus more for topping

½ tsp baking soda

½ tsp baking powder

1½ tsp cornstarch or arrowroot starch

1-3 Tbsp (15-45ml) unsweetened plain almond milk or DIY Almond Milk (page 6)

1 cup (180g) dairy-free dark or semisweet chocolate chips (or bar, chopped)

OPTIONAL
1 tsp coconut oil

01 Add the softened butter to large bowl. Cream using a standing mixer for 1 minute.

02 Add the peanut butter, cane sugar, brown sugar, and vanilla. Beat for 1 minute.

03 Add the pumpkin purée, then mix once more.

04 Set a sifter (see note) over something that will catch fallout (such as paper) and add the dry ingredients in this order: ½ cup (68g) flour, salt, baking soda, baking powder, cornstarch, and the remaining ¾ cup (102g) flour. Use a spoon to gently stir, then sift over the wet ingredients and beat to combine.

05 If the dough appears crumbly, add 1-3 Tbsp (15-45ml) almond milk until a dough is formed. Otherwise, skip this step.

06 Cover and freeze the dough for 20 minutes, or refrigerate for 35 minutes (or chill overnight).

07 Preheat the oven to 350 degrees F (176 degrees C). Position the rack in the center of the oven.

08 Scoop out roughly 2 Tbsp (36g) amounts of dough, and form into balls with the warmth of your hands. Gently press into loose discs with your palms.

continued

09 Use a fork to squish the cookies down a little more and form a crosshatch pattern on top. (For smaller cookies, scoop out heaping 1 Tbsp (20g) amounts and repeat the same process.)

10 Place the cookies on a baking sheet 2 inches apart to allow for spreading, and bake on the center rack for 12-16 minutes (or 8-10 minutes for smaller cookies), or until very slightly golden brown on the edges.

11 Remove from the oven and let rest on the baking sheet for 5 minutes, then transfer to a cooling rack to cool completely.

12 In the meantime, rinse and dry the large bowl and add the chocolate and coconut oil (optional). Melt in your microwave in 30-second increments (or over a double boiler), being careful not to overheat the mixture.

13 Line a clean plate or baking sheet with wax paper or parchment paper to receive the dipped cookies. Dip the cooled cookies halfway into the chocolate, gently shake off any excess, and place on the prepared surface. Sprinkle with sea salt (optional).

14 Let dry at room temperature until set. Serve the cookies chilled or at room temperature.

15 Store leftovers in a covered container in the refrigerator or at room temperature for up to 3 days, or freeze for up to 1 month. Best when fresh.

Notes

*To speed the softening process, slice the vegan butter into ¼-inch pieces.

*If you do not have pumpkin purée, substitute a comparable amount of applesauce or 1 prepared Flax Egg (page 6).

*If you do not own a sifter, simply whisk together the dry ingredients in a separate bowl, and add to wet ingredients as instructed.

Blackberry Custard Pie

This recipe is a crowd pleaser! I served it at a dinner party with friends, and it was gone before I could ask what everyone thought. The crust is gluten-free but can easily be modified if you don't need to eat gluten-free. The custard center is citrusy, perfectly sweet, and studded with blackberries. Serve this in the summer months when berries reach their peak ripeness.

SERVES 8	PREP TIME* 1 HR. 5 MIN. (+3–4 HRS. COOLING)	COOK TIME 1 HR. 10 MIN.	TOTAL TIME 2 HR. 15 MIN.

GLUTEN-FREE PIECRUST
1¼ cups (200g) Bob's Red Mill Gluten Free 1-to-1 Baking Flour (see note) or Gluten-Free Flour Blend (page 7)

¼ tsp sea salt

6 Tbsp (84g) cold vegan butter

5–7 Tbsp (75–105ml) ice-cold water

FILLING
1 8-ounce (227g) package plain vegan cream cheese

1 cup packed (248g) firm silken tofu (see note)

½ cup (120ml) maple syrup or agave nectar

2 lemons, juiced (~4 Tbsp or 60ml)

1 tsp pure vanilla extract

Pinch of sea salt

2 Tbsp (14g) cornstarch or arrowroot starch

1¼ cups (150g) blackberries, rinsed and well drained

OPTIONAL
Organic powdered sugar, for dusting the top

01 To prepare the crust, add the flour and salt to large bowl. Whisk to combine.

02 Slice or dollop the butter in and work with a fork or pastry cutter to cut it in until the mixture resembles wet sand.

03 Add ice-cold water 1 Tbsp (15ml) at a time, using a wooden spoon to stir. Add only as much water as is needed to help the mixture form a dough.

04 When a loose dough is formed, use your hands to shape it into a loose ball in the bowl. Transfer the dough to a piece of plastic wrap. Work the dough gently with your hands to form a ½-inch-thick disc and wrap firmly.

05 Refrigerate for 30 minutes (up to 2 days–just let it warm back up for 5-10 minutes before using). If the dough is too warm, it will be too soft to handle.

06 Once the dough is chilled, preheat the oven to 350 degrees F (176 degrees C) and prepare the pie filling.

07 Add the cream cheese, tofu, maple syrup, lemon juice, vanilla, salt, and cornstarch to the bowl of a blender. Blend until creamy and smooth, scraping down the sides as needed. Taste and adjust the flavors as needed, adding more lemon juice for acidity, maple syrup for sweetness, or salt for balance. Set aside.

continued

08 To roll out the crust, unwrap the disc and place it between two sizable pieces of wax paper or parchment paper. (Plastic wrap will work fine, but it is a little more difficult to manage.) Use a rolling pin to gently roll the crust into a circle slightly larger than your pie dish. If it cracks, don't stress—it can be re-formed with your hands once you get it in the pan, as the dough is fairly forgiving.

09 To transfer the crust, remove the top layer of wax paper. Gently lay the pie dish facedown on top of the crust. Working quickly, use the support of the wax paper to carefully invert it. Use your hands to gently form the dough into the pan, working it up along the sides.

10 Try not to overwork the dough in the process—it should not take more than a few minutes to perfect the shape. Any holes or cracks can be mended with a little excess dough and the heat of your hand.

11 I advise against trying to be fancy and doing any elaborate design with the crust. Just get the crust in, get a flat edge, and go.

12 Take a fork and puncture the bottom of the crust 5 or 6 times, then pour in the filling and smooth the top with a spoon. Top with the blackberries and very gently press the berries into the custard to settle.

13 Bake for 1 hour 5 minutes to 1 hour 15 minutes. The crust should be light golden brown, especially on the edges, and the filling should be a little jiggly in the center.

14 Remove from the oven and let cool completely—3-4 hours—before serving. As an optional touch, dust with organic powdered sugar. This pie is best at room temperature.

15 The pie will keep loosely covered for 2-3 days, though best when fresh. Loosely cover and refrigerate after one day.

Notes

*I often use Bob's Red Mill Gluten Free 1-to-1 Baking Flour in my piecrusts because I love its finely milled texture. However, if you cannot find it at the store, my Gluten-Free Flour Blend (page 7) works great as well.

*If not gluten-free, substitute unbleached all-purpose flour for the gluten-free blend. The dough will likely require less water, so be mindful to only add as much as needed.

*Be sure to use silken tofu for this recipe, or the texture will be less creamy and the taste will be negatively affected.

Blender Sweet Potato Pie

A sweet potato pie made in a blender? Absolutely! It's the lazy cook's dream. Make this for fall and holiday gatherings to wow your guests. This also works well with pumpkin purée if you do not happen to be into sweet potatoes.

SERVES 8

PREP TIME 15 MIN.* (+ CHILLING TIME)	COOK TIME 1 HR. 30 MIN.	TOTAL TIME 1 HR. 45 MIN.

FILLING
2½ pounds sweet potatoes (see note)

¼ cup (60ml) maple syrup

¼ cup (55g) organic brown sugar or coconut sugar, packed

½ cup (120ml) unsweetened plain almond milk or DIY Almond Milk (page 6), plus more as needed

1 Tbsp (15ml) olive oil

2½ Tbsp (17½g) cornstarch or arrowroot starch

1 tsp ground cinnamon

¼ tsp sea salt

CRUST
1½ cups (204g) all-purpose flour, plus more for dusting the surface, rolling pin, and dough (see note)

¼ tsp sea salt

7 Tbsp (98g) cold salted vegan butter, cut into chunks

2-5 Tbsp (30-75ml) ice-cold water

OPTIONAL
¼ tsp ground nutmeg

1 tsp pure vanilla extract

01 If using sweet potato or pumpkin purée, skip to step 04. Otherwise, add the sweet potatoes (skin on) to a large pot and cover with water.

02 Bring to a boil and cook for 15-20 minutes, or until very soft and the potatoes easily slide off a knife. Cook time varies depending on the size of the potato.

03 Remove the sweet potatoes from the pot and let them cool. Once cooled, remove the skin and set aside.

04 Make the crust. Preheat the oven to 350 degrees F (176 degrees C). Add the flour and salt to the bowl of a blender (or mixing bowl) and pulse (or whisk) to combine. Add the cold butter and pulse to combine (or cut in with a fork or pastry cutter). The texture should resemble wet sand.

05 With the blender on the lowest speed, add the water 1 Tbsp (15ml) at a time, until a loose dough is formed. Add only as much water as is needed to help the dough come together, or the crust will be tough.

06 Transfer the dough to a lightly floured surface. Work gently with your hands to form a ½-inch-thick disc.

continued

07 Lightly dust a rolling pin and the dough with flour. Roll into a circle just larger than the circumference of the pie pan, adding more flour if needed.

08 Using the rolling pin, gently the roll crust onto the pin. Then unroll and drape the crust over the pie dish. Try not to stretch the crust or it will shrink back during baking.

09 Crimp the edges of the crust into whatever design you wish. Then use a fork to poke a few holes into the bottom the of the crust.

10 To prepare the pie filling, add the peeled cooked sweet potatoes (or sweet potato purée) and the maple syrup, brown sugar, almond milk, olive oil, constarch, cinnamon, salt, nutmeg (optional), and vanilla (optional) to the bowl of a blender and blend until creamy and smooth, scraping down the sides as needed (or whisk/beat in a mixing bowl).

11 Taste and adjust the spices and sweetness as needed. Add more almond milk 1 Tbsp (15ml) at a time if the ingredients have trouble blending together. Pour the filling into the piecrust and even the top with a spoon.

12 Bake at 350 degrees F (176 degrees C) for 60-70 minutes. The crust should be light golden brown and the filling should be just a bit jiggly with some cracks on top.

13 Remove from the oven and let cool completely before loosely covering with a paper towel and foil (the paper towel will catch any moisture). Transfer to the refrigerator to set for 4-6 hours, preferably overnight.

14 Serve chilled or at room temperature with Coconut Whipped Cream (page 8), a sprinkle of cinnamon or nutmeg, and/or my Brown Sugar Pecans (page 11).

Notes

*For a faster prep, substitute sweet potatoes for 3 cups (600g) canned sweet potato or pumpkin purée.

*To keep this recipe gluten-free, substitute my Gluten-Free Flour Blend (page 7) or Bob's Red Mill Gluten Free 1-to-1 Baking Flour.

1-Bowl Vegan Tiramisu Cake

This recipe is adapted from my Vegan Funfetti Cupcakes on the blog. The twist is that it's made into a cake, brushed with bold coffee, and topped with a mascarpone-inspired whipped cream cheese frosting! One slice will not be enough. When you are craving tiramisu, this cake is the answer.

SERVES 9

| PREP TIME 1 HR. 15 MIN. | COOK TIME 50 MIN. | TOTAL TIME 2 HR. 5 MIN. |

1 cup (240ml) unsweetened plain almond milk or DIY Almond Milk (page 6)

1 tsp apple cider vinegar or lemon juice

½ cup (1 stick or 112g) softened vegan butter (see note)

¾ cup (150g) organic cane sugar

1 tsp pure vanilla extract

1¼ cups (170g) unbleached all-purpose flour

½ tsp baking soda

1½ tsp baking powder

2 Tbsp (14g) cornstarch or arrowroot starch

¼ tsp sea salt

⅓ cup (80ml) bold coffee, cooled

Vegan dark chocolate shavings or cocoa powder, for topping (optional)

continued

01 Preheat the oven to 350 degrees F (176 degrees C). Lightly grease an 8 × 8-inch baking dish.

02 In a liquid measuring cup, measure out the almond milk and add the vinegar. Let sit for 5 minutes.

03 Add the butter to a large bowl and cream using a standing mixer. Then add the sugar and vanilla and beat until fluffy, about 2 minutes.

04 Add the dry ingredients to a sifter (see note) in this order: 1 cup (136g) flour, baking soda, baking powder, cornstarch, salt, and remaining ¼ cup (34g) flour.

05 Sift the dry ingredients over the butter/sugar mixture while mixing, alternating with the almond milk mixture. Blend until well incorporated and no large lumps remain.

06 Pour the batter into the prepared baking dish. Bake on center rack of the oven for 45-52 minutes, or until a toothpick inserted into the center comes out clean. The cake should be a light golden brown color.

continued

FROSTING

1 14-ounce (414ml) can coconut cream (see note), chilled in refrigerator overnight

8 ounces (227g) vegan cream cheese, softened

¼ tsp pure vanilla extract

½ tsp apple cider vinegar or lemon juice

¾-1 cup (84-112g) organic powdered sugar

07 To make the frosting, wipe clean your mixing bowl and open the can of chilled coconut cream. Add the hardened cream to the bowl (leaving the clear liquid behind). Using a standing mixer, beat the coconut cream into airy peaks, then add cream cheese, vanilla, and vinegar. Mix.

08 Add the powdered sugar, ¼ cup (28g) at a time until the desired sweetness is reached. The mixture should be fairly thick but still spreadable. Put in the refrigerator to chill.

09 Once the cake is fully cooled, poke holes with a toothpick, skewer, or knife and brush generously with coffee. You want to add as much coffee as the cake will absorb. Stop when it no longer soaks easily into the top layer. You may not use all of the coffee.

10 Top the cake with the frosting and smooth with a spoon. Serve immediately, or loosely cover and chill anywhere from 4 hours to overnight. Garnish with chocolate shavings or cocoa powder if desired.

11 Leftovers will keep covered in the refrigerator 2-3 days, though the cake is best within the first 24 hours.

Notes

*To speed the softening process, slice the vegan butter into ¼-inch pieces.

*If you don't have a sifter, whisk together in a separate bowl.

*If you don't have coconut cream, coconut milk works as well. Chill, as instructed, overnight. When retrieved, make sure not to tip the can. Open the top and scoop out the hardened cream, leaving any clear liquid behind. There will be slightly less volume than the coconut cream yields, but it will still work.

Apricot Hand Pies

Can you believe I'd never cooked with apricots before making these hand pies? Now I'm in love! Enjoy these perfectly flaky, tart-sweet pies as a fruity dessert in the summertime. They are extra dreamy with some dairy-free ice cream. Keep them seasonal by swapping out whatever fruit is available near you.

YIELDS 10 HAND PIES

PREP TIME 25 MIN. | **COOK TIME 30 MIN.** | **TOTAL TIME 55 MIN.**

FILLING

5 ripe apricots (~400g with pits), pitted and cut into bite-size pieces

¼ cup (48g) coconut sugar (or substitute organic cane sugar), plus more to taste (see note)

1 Tbsp (7g) cornstarch or arrowroot starch

Pinch of sea salt

CRUST

2 cups (272g) unbleached all-purpose flour, plus more as needed

¼ tsp sea salt

⅔ cup (150g) cold vegan butter, plus melted vegan butter for the topping

5-7 Tbsp (75-105ml) ice-cold water

1 Tbsp (12½g) organic cane sugar, for the topping

01 Preheat the oven to 375 degrees F (190 degrees C). Line a rimmed baking sheet with parchment paper.

02 Prepare the apricot filling by placing the sliced apricots in a large bowl and adding the coconut sugar, cornstarch, and salt. Stir to combine, then set aside.

03 To prepare the crust, mix the flour and salt in a large bowl. Cut in the butter with fork or pastry cutter until well combined. The mixture should resemble wet sand.

04 Add cold water 1 Tbsp (15ml) at a time and mix with a wooden spoon until it forms a loose dough. It should be moist enough to form into a ball, but not too sticky to knead. Add more flour if it gets too wet.

05 Turn onto a well-floured surface, shape into a disc, and use a rolling pin to roll into a large circle, adding more flour as needed.

06 Place a small dish that is about 4 inches (10½cm) across (or a large round cookie cutter) over the dough and use a knife or pizza cutter to cut out circles—makes 9 or 10.

07 Re-form the dough scraps and roll back out until all of the dough is used (with the exception of a few scraps).

continued

08 Place 4 or 5 circles of dough on a parchment-lined baking sheet (leaving room to work). Use a slotted spoon to scoop modest amounts of filling on one half of each pie circle, leaving excess liquid behind. Then run a wet finger around edges to help them seal. Use your hands to gently fold the dough over.

09 Use a fork to seal the edges. Repeat until all of the filling is used and all of the pies are on the baking sheet.

10 Use a toothpick or small knife to poke a few holes in the top of each. Brush the tops of the pies with melted butter or coconut oil and sprinkle the tops with sugar. Bake for 25-35 minutes, or until golden brown.

11 Let cool for 5 minutes before serving. Let leftovers cool completely. Store in an airtight container at room temperature for up to 3 days. Best when fresh.

Note

*By nature, apricots are tart, so the pies are more on the tart than sweet side. To add more sweetness, substitute strawberries for up to half of the apricots, or add 1-2 Tbsp (12-24g) additional coconut sugar.

Pumpkin Apple Upside-Down Cake

This recipe was inspired by my love for fall and my 1-Bowl Gingerbread Cake from the blog. It's perfectly tender, subtly spiced, and it doesn't need icing, thanks to the layer of caramelized apples. This is a showstopping dessert that's perfect for fall and winter, and best when served with a dollop of Coconut Whipped Cream (page 8) and a dash of ground cinnamon.

SERVES 10

PREP TIME 15 MIN. | **COOK TIME 60 MIN.** | **TOTAL TIME 1 HR. 15 MIN.**

APPLES

1 large tart apple (Granny Smith is best)

3 Tbsp (41g) organic brown sugar, packed (or substitute coconut sugar)

Pinch of sea salt

½ tsp ground cinnamon

1 Tbsp (14g) cold vegan butter or coconut oil

CAKE

1 Flax Egg (page 6)

¾ cup (180ml) unsweetened plain almond milk or DIY Almond Milk (page 6) (substitute up to half with water)

¾ tsp freshly squeezed lemon juice or apple cider vinegar

1¼ tsp baking soda

3½ Tbsp (44g) organic cane sugar or coconut sugar

¼ cup (55g) organic brown sugar, packed

2 Tbsp (40g) blackstrap molasses (or substitute maple syrup)

continued

01 Preheat the oven to 350 degrees F (176 degrees C). Butter one 8-inch round (or similar size) cake pan, or an 8 × 8-inch baking dish. Add flour to coat, then shake out the excess and set aside.

02 Peel the apple, remove the core, quarter, and slice each quarter into 5 or 6 thin slices. Add the slices to a large bowl. Toss with brown sugar, salt, and cinnamon to coat.

03 Arrange the apple slices in bottom of the prepared cake pan in a fanned-out, circular shape. Cut the butter into small portions and place on top of the apples.

04 Bake for 12-14 minutes, or until bubbly and golden brown. Remove from the oven and reduce the oven heat to 325 degrees F (162 degrees C).

05 In the meantime, prepare the cake. In the same mixing bowl used earlier, prepare the flax egg. Let sit for 5 minutes.

06 Measure out the almond milk in a liquid measuring cup and add the lemon juice and baking soda. Whisk.

07 To the flax egg, add the cane sugar and brown sugar and whisk thoroughly. Then add the molasses, olive oil, vanilla, and pumpkin. Whisk again to combine. Last,

continued

¼ cup (60ml) olive oil, melted coconut oil, or melted vegan butter

¾ tsp pure vanilla extract

¾ cup (150g) pumpkin purée (not pumpkin pie filling)

1 cup (152g) whole wheat flour (see note)

1 tsp baking powder

½ tsp sea salt

½ tsp ground ginger

1 tsp ground cinnamon

⅓ cup (30g) rolled oats

add almond milk mixture and whisk again to combine.

08 Set a sifter over a towel or piece of paper to catch fallout (if you don't have a sifter, combine the ingredients in separate mixing bowl). Add the dry ingredients in this order: ¾ cup (114g) whole wheat flour, baking powder, salt, ginger, cinnamon, and the remaining ¼ cup (38g) whole wheat flour. Stir gently with a spoon, then sift over the wet ingredients. Stir to combine, being careful not to overmix.

09 Add the oats. Stir again until just combined. The batter should be thick but pourable. Pour over apples and spread into an even layer.

10 Bake on the center rack for 40-50 minutes. If using an 8 × 8-inch square dish, the baking time should be about the same.

11 When done, a toothpick inserted into the center should come out clean, and the edges should be visibly browned and dry. It's better to slightly overbake this cake than underbake, since the apples provide extra moisture. Remove from the oven and set on a counter to cool.

12 Once completely cooled, run a butter knife along the edge of the cake, then gently invert it onto a serving dish. For serving, this is delicious with dairy-free vanilla ice cream, Coconut Whipped Cream (page 8), or a dusting of organic powdered sugar.

13 Store leftovers covered at room temperature or in the refrigerator for up to 3 days.

Note

*To keep this cake gluten-free, replace the whole wheat flour with ¼ cup (27g) almond meal, ¼ cup (22g) gluten-free oat flour, and ½ (80g) cup Gluten-Free Flour Blend (page 7). Baking time may increase as gluten-free flours can take slightly longer to bake through.

Vegan Vanilla Cupcakes

This recipe took several attempts to perfect, but I'm supremely happy with the result. These vegan, gluten-free cupcakes are tender, perfectly sweet, and surprisingly simple to make. Top with vegan buttercream frosting to take these beauties to the next level.

SERVES 12

| PREP TIME 15 MIN. | COOK TIME 25 MIN. | TOTAL TIME 40 MIN. |

Scant ½ cup (115ml) unsweetened plain almond milk or DIY Almond Milk (page 6)

¾ tsp apple cider vinegar or lemon juice

1½ tsp baking soda

2 Flax Eggs (page 6)

½ cup (100g) organic cane sugar

¼ cup plus 1 Tbsp (75ml) maple syrup or agave nectar

¾ cup (184g) unsweetened applesauce

½ cup (120ml) melted coconut oil, grape seed oil, or melted vegan butter

1 tsp pure vanilla extract

½ tsp baking powder

¼ tsp sea salt

⅔ cup (73g) almond meal, plus more as needed

⅓ cup (30g) gluten-free oat flour

continued

01 Preheat the oven to 350 degrees F (176 degrees C). Line 12 muffin tins with paper liners, or lightly grease and flour (with gluten-free flour). Shake out excess.

02 In a liquid measuring cup, measure out the almond milk, add the vinegar and baking soda, and stir. Let sit for 5 minutes.

03 In the meantime, prepare the flax eggs in a large bowl. Let sit for 5 minutes.

04 Add the sugar, maple syrup, and almond milk mixture to the Flax Eggs and beat to combine. Then add the applesauce, coconut oil, vanilla, baking powder, and salt. Mix.

05 Add the almond meal, oat flour, and Gluten-Free Flour Blend. Beat or whisk to combine. If the batter appears too thick, add a little almond milk. If too thin, add a little more Gluten-Free Flour Blend or almond meal. The batter should be thin but pourable.

06 Divide the batter evenly among the muffin tins, filling them ¾ full (there should be enough for 11 or 12 cupcakes). Bake for 24-31 minutes or until puffy, golden brown, and a toothpick inserted into the center comes out completely clean.

continued

1 cup (160g) Gluten-Free
Flour Blend (page 7) or
Bob's Red Mill 1-to-1
Gluten Free Baking Flour,
plus more as needed

FROSTING

½ cup (112g) vegan
butter, softened (see
note)

½ tsp vanilla extract

1¼-2 cups (140-224g)
organic powdered sugar

1-3 Tbsp (15-45ml)
unsweetened plain almond
milk or DIY Almond milk
(page 6) (to thin)

07 Remove from the oven and let rest
in the muffin tin for 10-15 minutes,
then remove and let cool completely on a
cooling rack. Allow the cupcakes to fully
cool before unwrapping to avoid them
sticking to the wrappers.

08 For the frosting, wipe/rinse your
mixing bowl clean and add the butter and
vanilla. Beat until light and fluffy. Then
add the powdered sugar ½ cup (56g) at a
time. Continue mixing until thick
and creamy.

09 Drizzle in a little almond milk to
thin. The frosting should be fairly
thick so as to hold its shape once on
the cupcakes, so only add as much milk as
necessary to make it spreadable. Add more
powdered sugar if it gets too thin.

10 Frost the cupcakes generously.
Sprinkles or fresh raspberries make the
perfect garnish.

11 Leftovers keep covered at room
temperature for up to 3 days, though
best within 24 hours.

Note

*To speed the softening process, slice the vegan
butter into ¼-inch pieces.

Strawberry Swirl Ice Cream

I'm not typically a fruit-in-my-dessert kind of girl, but when strawberries are involved I make exceptions. This creamy, perfectly sweet ice cream is infused with fresh strawberries in both blending and churning to give it an extra fruity edge. Enjoy this classic ice cream as is or with summer pies. Or turn it into a vegan milk shake.

SERVES 8

PREP TIME 2 HR. | **TOTAL TIME 2 HR. (+ FREEZING)**

1½ cups (180g) raw cashews

1½ cups (180g) ripe strawberries, hulled and chopped

1-2 Tbsp (12-25g) organic cane sugar, plus more as needed

¼ cup (60ml) olive oil or melted coconut oil

1 tsp pure vanilla extract

1 cup (236ml) full-fat or light coconut milk (or substitute unsweetened plain almond milk or DIY Almond milk on page 6), plus more as needed

½ cup (120ml) maple syrup (substitute up to half with organic cane sugar)

01 The night or day before, place your ice cream maker bowl in the freezer to chill. Also, quick-soak the cashews (see page 15).

02 While the cashews are soaking, add the strawberries and sugar to a medium bowl and stir/mash to combine. Adjust the amount of sugar according to taste, adding more if the strawberries are not very sweet. Set aside.

03 Once the cashews are soaked, drain and add to the bowl of a blender with the olive oil, vanilla, coconut milk, maple syrup, and half the strawberries. Blend until smooth. If there is trouble blending, add more coconut milk. Taste and adjust the flavor as needed, adding more sweetener if desired.

04 Transfer the mixture to a large bowl and cover. Chill in the refrigerator overnight (or at least 4-6 hours). Also cover the remaining strawberries and put them in the refrigerator.

05 The following day, pour the chilled mixture into the ice cream churner and churn according to the manufacturer's instructions until a thick soft serve is reached, about 30 minutes. Toward the end of the churning, add the remaining strawberries and turn off the machine when ice cream is slightly swirled.

continued

06 Transfer the mixture to a freezer-safe container and cover securely. Freeze for 4-6 hours, or until firm. Thaw for at least 15 minutes before scooping. Use a hot scoop to ease serving. Will keep for about 1 week in the freezer, though best when fresh.

Peanut Butter + Jelly Ice Cream Sandwiches

A peanut butter and jelly sandwich in dessert form. How could you go wrong? These easy-to-make ice cream sandwiches are possible thanks to no-bake peanut butter cookies and generous scoops of my Strawberry Swirl Ice Cream (page 244). Creamy, tender, and perfectly salty-sweet.

SERVES 7
(14 COOKIES, 7 SANDWICHES)

PREP TIME 2 HR. 30 MIN. | TOTAL TIME 2 HR. 30 MIN.

NO-BAKE PEANUT BUTTER COOKIES
1 cup (140g) roasted lightly salted peanuts (if unsalted, add a pinch more salt)

½ cup (56g) raw almonds

⅓ cup dates (~6 dates or 67g), pitted

½ cup (128g) salted creamy peanut butter

Sea salt to taste and for the topping (depending on the saltiness of peanuts/peanut butter)

SANDWICHES
1¾ cups (~350g) Strawberry Swirl Ice Cream (page 244)

01 Add the peanuts and almonds to the bowl of a food processor or high-speed blender and grind into a meal. Remove and set aside.

02 Add the dates to the bowl of a food processor or blender and pulse until small bits remain (or it forms a ball). Add the peanut butter and nut meal, and pulse to combine, scraping down the sides as needed. Taste and adjust the flavor as needed, adding more salt if desired.

03 Scoop out heaping 1 Tbsp (~22g) amounts of dough to make about 14 cookies. Use your hands to roll the dough into balls. Place them on a parchment-lined baking sheet or plate and gently smash down with a fork, making crosshatch marks on the tops. Sprinkle with a little salt (optional). Place in the freezer to firm for 1 hour.

04 To assemble the sandwiches, thaw the strawberry ice cream at room temperature for 15 minutes. Scoop out ¼ cup (~50g) amounts.

05 Add the ice cream to the bottom side of one peanut butter cookie. Top with another cookie, pressing down slightly to seal.

06 Repeat until all of the sandwiches are assembled, then immediately transfer to the freezer to avoid melting. Freeze until firm, about 1 hour. Serve right out of the freezer or let thaw 5 minutes to soften.

Cherry Chia Lassi Pops

I couldn't help but wonder what would happen if I froze a cherry lassi. The results were delicious! These creamy, cherry-filled pops make the perfect summer dessert and are a great recipe to prepare with kids!

YIELDS ~10 LASSI POPS

PREP TIME 10 MIN. + FREEZING TIME

TOTAL TIME 10 MIN.

12 ounces (340g) vegan vanilla or cherry-flavored yogurt (see note)

½ cup (118ml) light coconut milk, plain unsweetened almond milk, or DIY Almond milk, (page 6)

⅔ cup (~93g) pitted sweet red cherries, chopped (fresh or frozen)

1 Tbsp (12g) chia seeds

OPTIONAL
1-2 Tbsp (15-30ml) maple syrup or coconut sugar

01 Add the yogurt, coconut milk, maple syrup (optional), and half the cherries to the bowl of a blender. Purée until creamy and smooth.

02 Add the remaining cherries and chia seeds. Pulse to just combine—there should be some chunky pieces remaining.

03 Pour into Popsicle molds. The recipe should yield 8 large pops or 12-14 small pops, depending on the size of the molds.

04 Freeze until firm, at least 4-6 hours, and enjoy! Best within 5-7 days.

Note

*Soy cherry yogurt is an ideal flavor, though vanilla soy or coconut work here, too.

Peanut Butter Fudge Swirl Ice Cream

I've been dreaming of a peanut butter fudge vegan ice cream for years, and this one finally fits the bill. The creamy, custard base is infused with salty peanut butter, and a chocolate ganache ripple takes this ice cream to the next level. Serve as is, or make it a sundae with Coconut Whipped Cream (page 8), salted nuts, and a generous drizzle of my Coconut Sugar Caramel Sauce (page 265).

SERVES 7	PREP TIME 1 HR. 50 MIN	COOK TIME 8 MIN.	TOTAL TIME 1 HR. 58 MIN. (+ FREEZING TIME)

ICE CREAM

1 cup (120g) raw cashews

14 ounces (414ml) full-fat coconut milk (substitute light for less creamy results)

¼ cup (60ml) maple syrup

¼ cup (50g) organic cane sugar

½ cup (128g) natural salted peanut butter, crunchy or creamy

2 Tbsp (30ml) olive oil or melted coconut oil

1 tsp pure vanilla extract

Pinch of sea salt (optional), plus more to taste

CHOCOLATE GANACHE

⅔ cup (80g) vegan dark chocolate (not chips), chopped

¼ cup (60ml) plain unsweetened almond milk or coconut milk, or DIY Almond Milk (page 6)

2 Tbsp (14g) icing/organic powdered sugar (optional)

ICE CREAM

01 The night before, place the ice cream churning bowl in the freezer to chill.

02 Quick-soak the cashews (see page 15). While the cashews soak, prepare the base by adding the coconut milk, maple syrup, sugar, peanut butter, and olive oil to a small saucepan over medium heat. Whisk to combine.

03 Cook until the mixture just begins to simmer, 4-5 minutes. Remove from the heat. Add the vanilla and salt (optional). Whisk once more. Set aside.

04 Add the mixture to the bowl of a blender with the soaked, drained cashews and blend until creamy and smooth, about 3-4 minutes, scraping down the sides as needed. The mixture should be completely creamy and blended.

05 Taste and adjust the flavor as needed. I add a pinch of salt to enhance the peanut butter flavor.

06 Transfer the mixture to a large bowl and cover. Put it in the refrigerator to chill overnight (or at least 4-6 hours).

continued

07 The following day, prepare the chocolate ganache by placing the chopped chocolate in a medium bowl. In a separate bowl, heat the almond milk in your microwave for 1 minute. Alternatively, heat the almond milk in a saucepan until just simmering.

08 Add the heated almond milk to the chopped chocolate. Let sit for 5 minutes, covered, to allow the chocolate to melt. Do not touch.

09 After 5 minutes, stir to incorporate. If clumps remain, microwave the mixture for 10-20 seconds, or until completely smooth.

10 Add the powdered sugar and whisk to combine, making sure no clumps remain. Set aside to cool.

11 Add the chilled ice cream base to the chilled churning bowl and churn according to manufacturer's instructions, about 30 minutes. It should resemble soft serve.

12 If for some reason it doesn't thicken up, place the mixture (still in the churning bowl) back in the freezer for 30-40 minutes to thicken before churning once more.

13 Once the ice cream has the consistency of soft serve, add the ganache and churn only until it's slightly incorporated to achieve a swirl. Turn off the machine.

14 Transfer the ice cream to a freezer-safe container and smooth it with a spoon. Cover securely and freeze for at least 4-6 hours, or until firm.

15 Let sit a room temperature for 20-30 minutes before serving, to soften. Use a hot scoop to ease serving. Will keep for up to 1 week in the freezer.

Double Chocolate Skillet Bread Pudding

When I took my first bite of this experimental dessert, I squealed. I didn't know if tofu would work in the same way eggs do in traditional bread pudding, and I was so pleasantly surprised when the answer was a resounding yes! This bread pudding is tender on the inside, crisp on the outside, and loaded with chocolate flavor. Serve this crowd-pleasing dessert at holiday gatherings or dinner parties with a little Coconut Whipped Cream (page 8), dairy-free ice cream, or my Coconut Sugar Caramel Sauce (page 265)!

SERVES 6

PREP TIME 2 HR. 15 MIN.	COOK TIME 50 MIN.	TOTAL TIME 3 HR. 5 MIN.

1½ Tbsp (22ml) coconut oil (or substitute vegan butter)

12 ounces (340g) stale/dry white or wheat bread (rustic loaves are best)

¾ cup (90g) vegan dark or bittersweet chocolate, chopped

8 ounces (226g) silken extra-firm tofu, patted dry (see note)

1 cup (240ml) unsweetened plain almond milk or DIY Almond milk (page 6)

¼ cup (24g) unsweetened cocoa powder or cacao powder

½ cup (96g) coconut sugar (or substitute organic cane sugar), plus more for topping

1 Tbsp (7g) cornstarch or arrowroot starch

3 Tbsp (45g) coconut cream or full-fat coconut milk

1 tsp pure vanilla extract

01 Use 1 Tbsp (15ml) coconut oil to generously grease a 12-inch cast-iron skillet or 8 × 8-inch baking dish.

02 Slice or tear the bread into ½-inch cubes and add to the skillet. Top with chopped chocolate and spread to distribute.

03 Add the remaining ingredients to the bowl of a blender and purée until smooth. Taste and adjust the flavor as needed, adding more cocoa powder powder to enhance the chocolate flavor, or coconut sugar for sweetness, then pour over the bread.

04 Cover and let soak for 2 hours at room temperature or overnight (6-8 hours) in the refrigerator, periodically poking down or turning over any pieces of bread that are above the liquid and appear dry.

05 Preheat oven to 325 degrees F (162 degrees C). Bake for 40-45 minutes or until the top has some color and the center is no longer wet.

06 Remove from the oven and turn the oven to low broil. Spray or brush the top of the bread pudding with ½ Tbsp (7½ml) melted coconut oil and sprinkle with 1 Tbsp more coconut sugar.

continued

07 Return to the oven on the middle rack for 1-2 minutes, watching closely, or until the top is nice and crusty. Do not walk away as to ensure it doesn't burn.

08 Let cool 5-10 minutes before serving. Serve as is, with dairy-free ice cream, or with Coconut Whipped Cream (page 8).

Notes

*Be sure to use silken tofu for this recipe, or the texture will not get as creamy and smooth.

*Recipe adapted from Alton Brown.

Peanut Butter Cup Puffed Rice Bars

This may just be my new favorite candy bar. Salty peanut butter is naturally sweetened with dates and maple syrup, then tossed with puffed brown rice for a slightly crispy center. Packed and layered with generous coats of vegan dark chocolate, this is homemade candy bar making at its finest.

SERVES 16

PREP TIME 25 MIN. | **COOK TIME 5 MIN.** | **TOTAL TIME 30 MIN.**

1 cup (256g) salted natural peanut butter (or substitute cashew butter or almond butter)

½ cup (120ml) maple syrup

¼ cup (50g) packed finely chopped pitted dates (~5 large dates)

3½ cups (56g) puffed brown rice

2 Tbsp (14g) roasted unsalted sunflower seeds

1 cup (120g) vegan dark chocolate, chopped (70% cacao and above)

01 Line an 8 × 8-inch (or similar size) baking dish with parchment paper or plastic wrap.

02 Add the peanut butter and maple syrup to a small saucepan over medium-low heat. Stir to combine. Transfer to a large bowl and add the chopped dates.

03 Use a wooden spoon to mix/mash. Add the puffed rice and sunflower seeds and mix until the dry and wet ingredients are well incorporated.

04 Transfer the mixture to the prepared baking dish, and spread into an even layer. Lay a piece of plastic wrap or parchment on top and use a flat object—such as a drinking glass—or your hands to press down into an even, very compact bar.

05 Place the mixture in the freezer to firm for 10-15 minutes. In the meantime, heat the chocolate over a double boiler or in your microwave in 30-second increments. Set aside.

06 Remove the mixture from the freezer and lift it from the baking dish. Transfer it to a parchment-lined baking sheet.

07 Drizzle on the majority of the chocolate—about three-fourths—and use a brush or small spoon to spread the chocolate into an even, solid layer.

continued

08 Return the mixture to the freezer to set for 15 minutes. Then remove it, gently flip it over, and drizzle the top with the remaining chocolate.

09 Return the mixture to the freezer for 10 minutes or until the chocolate is firm. Then chop it into 16 (or desired number) bars.

10 Store leftovers in an airtight container in the refrigerator for 3-4 days, or in the freezer for up to 1 month.

No-Bake Strawberry Cheesecake Bars

These bars taste as delicious as they look. They are a spin on my favorite 7-Ingredient Cheesecake Bites from the blog, with an extra boost of lemon flavor and a perfectly tender, date-walnut crust. Strawberry compote makes an elegant, tart-sweet sauce for serving.

SERVES 12	PREP TIME 1 HR. 30 MIN.	COOK TIME 7 MIN.	TOTAL TIME 1 HR. 37 MIN. + FREEZING

CRUST
1 cup (~22 dates or 200g) packed dates, pitted (pitted before measuring), plus more as needed

1½ cups (180g) raw walnuts, plus more as needed

Pinch of sea salt (optional)

FILLING
1½ cups (180g) raw cashews, soaked (see note) and drained

1 cup (236ml) full-fat or light coconut milk (or substitute plain unsweetened almond milk or DIY Almond Milk on page 6 for less creamy results), plus more as needed

½ tsp pure vanilla extract

½ cup (120ml) maple syrup (substitute up to half with organic cane sugar), plus more as needed

3 Tbsp (45ml) olive oil or melted coconut oil, plus more as needed

1 lemon, zested (1 tsp) and juiced (2 Tbsp or 30ml), plus more lemon juice as needed

continued

01 Add the dates to the bowl of a food processor or blender and blend until small bits remain, or the mixture forms a ball. Remove and set aside.

02 Add walnuts and salt (optional) to the bowl of the food processor or blender and process into a meal. Add the dates back in, small chunks at a time, and process until a loose dough forms—it should stick together when squeezed between your fingers. If too dry, add a few more dates. If too wet, add more walnut meal.

03 Line an 8 × 8-inch (or similar size) baking dish with parchment paper or plastic wrap and add the crust. Spread in an even layer and press down with your hands for a uniformly flat crust. Place in the freezer to set.

04 In the meantime, add the cashews, coconut milk, vanilla, maple syrup, olive oil, lemon zest, lemon juice, and salt to the bowl of a blender.

05 Blend on high until puréed, creamy, and smooth. If there is trouble blending, add a bit more liquid (either coconut milk or olive oil) to help the process along. Scrape down the sides as needed. Taste and adjust the flavors as needed, adding more maple syrup for sweetness, or lemon juice for acidity.

continued

STRAWBERRY TOPPING

2 cups (240g) frozen strawberries (or substitute fresh strawberries, hulled and chopped)

1-2 Tbsp (15-30ml) maple syrup (or substitute coconut sugar or organic cane sugar), plus more to taste

1 Tbsp (7g) cornstarch or arrowroot starch

2-3 Tbsp (30-45ml) water (or substitute freshly squeezed orange juice)

06 Remove the crust from the freezer and pour the cashew mixture over the crust. Tap to remove air bubbles and smooth the top with a spoon. Loosely cover with plastic wrap and return to the freezer to harden, 3-4 hours. The cheesecake will mostly keep its form in the refrigerator, but freezing will expedite the "setting" process and make slicing easier.

07 In the meantime, prepare the strawberry topping. Add the strawberries, maple syrup, cornstarch, and a bit of water to a small saucepan over medium heat.

08 Cook for 2-3 minutes, then reduce the heat and begin mashing the strawberries with a spoon to break them into smaller pieces. Cook for 3-4 minutes more, then turn off heat to let cool and thicken, stirring occasionally. Transfer to a small bowl and cover. Refrigerate to cool completely.

09 Spread the chilled strawberry topping over the hardened cheesecake (or serve separately), slice into bars, and serve. Coconut Whipped Cream (page 8) makes an excellent topping.

10 Store leftovers in the refrigerator covered for 2-3 days, or in the freezer for up to 1 month. If frozen, let thaw for 15-20 minutes to soften before serving.

Note

*Soak the cashews for 6-8 hours in cool water, or pour boiling water over cashews and let rest uncovered at room temperature for 1 hour. Drain and proceed with the recipe as instructed.

Cherry Chocolate Chip Ice Cream

I've never been the type to choose cherry ice cream, but this recipe has me changing my mind. The vanilla–custard base pairs perfectly with sweet red cherries that have been cooked down into a compote. The dark chocolate flecks add a sophisticated, sweet finish.

SERVES 10	PREP TIME 1 HR. 15 MIN.	COOK TIME 5 MIN.	TOTAL TIME 1 HR. 20 MIN. + FREEZING

1½ cups (180g) raw cashews, soaked and drained (see note)

14 ounces (414ml) full-fat coconut milk (or light coconut milk with less creamy results)

3 Tbsp (45ml) olive oil or melted coconut oil

½ cup (120ml) maple syrup (substitute up to half with organic cane sugar), plus more as needed

1 tsp pure vanilla extract

Pinch of sea salt

1 Tbsp (8g) cornstarch or arrowroot starch

COMPOTE
1 cup (140g) sweet red cherries, pitted and halved (fresh or frozen)

1-2 Tbsp (15-30ml) freshly squeezed orange juice, or filtered water

1 Tbsp (15-30ml) maple syrup (or substitute organic cane or coconut sugar)

½ Tbsp (4g) cornstarch or arrowroot starch

⅓ cup (40g) vegan dark or semisweet chocolate, very finely chopped

01 The night before, place the ice cream churning bowl in the freezer to chill.

02 Add the cashews, coconut milk, olive oil, maple syrup, vanilla, salt, and cornstarch to the bowl of a high-speed blender. Blend until creamy and smooth, scraping down the sides as needed.

03 Taste and adjust the sweetness as needed, adding more sweetener if desired. I found ¼ cup (60ml) maple syrup and ¼ cup (50g) organic cane sugar to be perfect. Transfer to a medium mixing bowl and cover. For best results, chill overnight (or at least 5-6 hours).

04 The following day, prepare the compote by adding the cherries, orange juice, maple sugar, and cornstarch to a small saucepan. Bring to a simmer over medium heat and use a wooden spoon to slightly smash the cherries. Stir to incorporate.

05 Reduce the heat to low and let simmer for 3-4 minutes, until the mixture resembles cherry pie filling. Transfer to a clean bowl and cover to chill in the refrigerator while the ice cream churns.

06 Assemble the chilled ice cream maker and add the chilled ice cream batter. Churn until creamy and thick and the mixture resembles soft serve, about 30 minutes.

continued

07 In the last 30 seconds of churning, add the chilled cherry compote and chopped chocolate. Churn until just incorporated and slightly swirled. Turn off the machine. Transfer the ice cream to a freezer-safe container and smooth the top with a spoon.

08 Cover securely and freeze for 4-5 hours, or until firm. Before scooping, allow to sit at room temperature for 10-15 minutes to soften. Use a hot scoop to ease serving.

09 Leftovers keep in the freezer up to 1 week, though best within the first 2-3 days.

Note

*To quick-soak the cashews, place the cashews in a bowl and cover with boiling water. Let rest uncovered at room temperature for 1 hour, then drain thoroughly and proceed with the recipe as instructed.

Coconut Sugar Caramel Sauce

Perfecting vegan caramel has been such a challenge for me, but this recipe is exactly what I have been looking for! It's entirely gluten-free and naturally sweetened, and requires just 5 ingredients. Serve this warm or chilled with your favorite desserts, coffee beverages, and more. It pairs perfectly with my Cherry Chocolate Chip Ice Cream (page 261).

SERVES 16

PREP TIME 5 MIN. | **COOK TIME 15 MIN.** | **TOTAL TIME 20 MIN.**

1 cup (192g) coconut sugar

¼ cup (60ml) filtered water

½ tsp pure vanilla extract

¼ tsp sea salt

⅔ cup (160ml) coconut cream (not coconut milk)

OPTIONAL
1 Tbsp (15ml) bourbon (omit to keep gluten-free)

01 Place the coconut sugar and water in a small saucepan. Cook over medium heat for 9-11 minutes, swirling the pan but not stirring. Reduce the heat slightly if the mixture is bubbling too rapidly (and remove it from the heat if it begins smelling burnt). When caramelized, it will have a strong caramel scent and a dark amber color.

02 Once finished cooking, remove the pan from the heat and immediately add the vanilla, salt, and coconut cream. Stir to combine. Add the bourbon and stir again (optional). Let cool slightly, then transfer to a clean mason jar and let cool completely before covering/sealing.

03 Store in the refrigerator for 2-3 weeks. Reheat in your microwave, or place the jar in a saucepan with 2 inches of simmering water until warmed through. However, the sauce is also pourable and delicious directly from the refrigerator.

04 This caramel makes a great addition to vegan shakes, sundaes, and pies.

FRESH-PRESSED APPLE CIDER, PAGE 270

Beverages

IF YOU'VE COOKED YOUR WAY THROUGH THIS BOOK, IF YOU'RE FEELING parched after one too many veggie burgers, or if you're simply in the mood for a good drink, this section is for you.

Though modest, it has my five essentials: boozy, sweet, spicy, bubbly, and rich. Kick back, relax, and celebrate all that you've accomplished. Cheers, friends!

Pumpkin Chai Tea Lattes

If you follow Minimalist Baker online, you know I have a mild obsession with chai lattes. Well, this recipe may just be my favorite yet! I love how the pumpkin purée adds a rich, creamy texture and the spices add an earthy warmth. Enjoy this in the fall and winter, especially on chilly evenings. It's the perfect soul-warming beverage.

SERVES 2

PREP TIME 5 MIN. | **COOK TIME 15 MIN.** | **TOTAL TIME 20 MIN.**

2 cups (480ml) unsweetened plain almond milk or DIY Almond Milk (page 6)

1 cup (240ml) filtered water (for a super-creamy latte, replace with almond milk)

1 Tbsp-size piece of fresh ginger (or 1 tsp ground ginger)

¼ cup plus 1 Tbsp (62½g) unsweetened pumpkin purée

3 black or chai tea bags (see note)

3-4 Tbsp (21-28g) coconut sugar (or maple syrup), plus more as needed

Pinch each of sea salt and black pepper

½ tsp ground cinnamon, plus more as needed

¾ tsp pumpkin pie spice, plus more as needed

⅛ tsp ground ginger (optional), plus more as needed

Pinch of ground nutmeg

½ tsp cornstarch or arrowroot starch, for thickening (optional)

FOR SERVING
Coconut Whipped Cream (page 8)

Ground cinnamon

01 Add the almond milk, water, and ginger to a small saucepan. Warm over medium heat. Upon reaching a low boil, remove from the heat, whisk in the pumpkin purée, and drop in the tea bags.

02 Let steep for 10 minutes, then remove the ginger and tea bags. Thoroughly squeeze any leftover tea from the tea bags for maximum flavor.

03 Add the remaining ingredients (off heat) and whisk vigorously to combine. Taste and adjust the seasonings as needed. I add more sweetener and ground ginger.

04 Reheat slightly over medium-low heat until the preferred temperature is reached. Then serve with Coconut Whipped Cream (page 8) and additional pumpkin pie spice or cinnamon. Best when fresh.

Note

*If you are using chai tea bags, less ground seasonings may be required.

Fresh-Pressed Apple Cider

Who would've thought making your own apple cider at home could be so simple *and* wouldn't require any special equipment? If you have a blender and a kitchen towel, you can make this recipe. Want a bonus? You can either leave it as fresh-pressed apple juice to enjoy with breakfast or transform it into a subtly spiced cider—perfect for entertaining in the fall.

SERVES 9

| PREP TIME 10 MIN. | COOK TIME 20 MIN. | TOTAL TIME 30 MIN. |

9 or 10 medium apples
(3 pounds or 13-60g),
quartered, cored, skin on

2 cups (480ml)
filtered water, plus
more as needed

1-2 Tbsp (12-24g)
coconut sugar (or
maple syrup), more or
less depending on the
sweetness of the apples

1 lemon, juiced
(2 Tbsp or 30ml), plus
more as needed

2-3 cinnamon sticks, plus
more for garnish

Pinch of sea salt

01 Add the apples and water to the bowl of a blender. Blend on high speed until completely smooth and puréed. Depending on the size of the blender, this may need to be done in two batches.

02 Drape a large, thin dish towel over a large bowl, making sure the bowl is completely covered to prevent spillover.

03 Carefully pour the apple mixture onto the towel. Gather the corners of the towel and lift. Begin squeezing/twisting the towel to press out the juice. Continue until all that remains is pulp, which can be saved and added to smoothies or baked goods, or composted.

04 The result is fresh-pressed apple juice, which can be enjoyed as is, chilled, or made into apple cider.

05 To make cider, pour the juice into a large saucepan or pot. Add the coconut sugar, lemon juice, cinnamon sticks, and salt. Stir to combine and bring to a low boil over medium-high heat.

06 Once boiling, reduce the heat to low and simmer until the flavor of the cinnamon sticks has infused the juice, 15-20 minutes.

07 Taste and adjust the flavor as needed, adding more lemon for acidity, more coconut sugar for sweetness, or more cinnamon sticks for spice.

08 Serve hot with cinnamon sticks for a garnish. Add a dash of bourbon to make this a boozy hot toddy. Keep the cider warm over low heat if entertaining, and store cooled leftovers covered in the refrigerator for up to 1 week.

Creamy Vegan Eggnog

If you love ice cream, you'll love this festive beverage. It tastes like melted vanilla ice cream infused with warm, fall spices. It's rich, creamy, and flavorful, and perfect for holiday gatherings. No one will guess it's dairy-free!

SERVES 9

PREP TIME 1 HR. 10 MIN. | **TOTAL TIME 1 HR. 10 MIN.**

1½ cups (180g) raw cashews, quick-soaked (see note on page 72)

2¼ cups (540ml) unsweetened plain almond milk or DIY Almond Milk (page 6)

½ cup (118ml) light coconut milk

1 cup (240ml) filtered water, plus more to thin

6-8 Tbsp (90-120ml) maple syrup (substitute up to half with coconut sugar), plus more to taste

Healthy pinch of sea salt

¼ tsp ground cinnamon, plus more to taste

⅛ tsp ground nutmeg, plus more to taste

2 ounces (59ml) bourbon (optional, not gluten-free)

01 Add all of the ingredients except the bourbon to the bowl of a blender. Blend on high until creamy and smooth, scraping down the sides as needed. If there is trouble blending, add more water. The mixture should be extremely creamy, so blend on high for 2-3 minutes.

02 Taste and adjust the flavor as needed, adding more spices for warmth or maple syrup for sweetness.

03 Add the bourbon 1 ounce at a time. Blend and taste to determine your preference. This is optional, but a delicious addition!

04 If the blender does not get the mixture completely smooth and drinkable, strain through cheesecloth or a thin dish towel to remove cashew fragments before proceeding.

05 Eggnog can be enjoyed immediately over ice, or chilled (as I prefer it). To chill, transfer the mixture to a large pitcher. Cover and chill in the refrigerator for 6-8 hours or overnight. The flavors will develop and deepen the longer it rests.

06 Serve as is or with Coconut Whipped Cream (page 8) and a pinch more cinnamon or nutmeg. It will keep covered in the refrigerator for 4-6 days.

Simple Tamarind Whiskey Sour

This recipe pays homage to the best whiskey sour I've ever had, served at the Whiskey Soda Lounge in Portland, Oregon. The tamarind adds a slightly bitter and sour note, which plays well with the fresh lime juice. Cane sugar adds a sweet finish, and the bourbon punches through without overpowering the other flavors. It's dreamy. This is the perfect drink to make when you're entertaining friends during the summer, and pairs especially well with spicy dishes.

SERVES 1

PREP TIME 5 MIN. | **TOTAL TIME 5 MIN.**

Orange peel and maraschino cherry, for garnish

1½ Tbsp (19g) organic cane sugar (or substitute agave nectar or maple syrup)

1 ounce (2 Tbsp or 30ml) freshly squeezed lime or lemon juice

1 Tbsp (15g) fresh tamarind concentrate or paste (see note)

1½ ounces (44ml) bourbon whiskey (see note)

Ice, for shaking and serving

01 Prepare a glass with one large ice cube (or 4-6 small ice cubes), orange peel, and cherry. Set aside.

02 In a cocktail shaker, muddle the sugar, lime juice, and tamarind concentrate until well combined.

03 Add the bourbon and a generous handful of ice. Shake vigorously.

04 Pour over the ice and serve.

Notes

*Tamarind concentrate can be found online and in Asian grocery stores. It may seem like a rare ingredient, but I always have some on hand for cooking Asian dishes, especially pad Thai (see Peanut Butter Pad Thai on page 195).

*Ensure bourbon whiskey is gluten-free.

Sparkling Peach + Berry White Sangria

When we visited Spain in 2013, I fell in love with sangria. This recipe is an unexpected take on the classic drink, and uses sparkling white wine for a festive spin. Enjoy this on warm summer afternoons or with Spanish-inspired entrées.

SERVES 4

PREP TIME 10 MIN. | **TOTAL TIME 10 MIN.**

3-4 ounces (88-118ml) orange liqueur (such as Grand Marnier)

1 ripe peach, pitted and sliced

4 small strawberries, hulled, quartered

1 small handful of blueberries

1 kiwi, skin removed, sliced

½ orange, sliced, then quartered

1 750ml bottle dry sparkling white wine, chilled

OPTIONAL
1 sprig of fresh mint, for garnish

01 Add the orange liqueur, peach, strawberries, blueberries, kiwi, and orange to the pitcher. Stir.

02 Top with sparkling white wine and stir gently once more to mix.

03 Serve immediately. Garnish with mint if desired.

Minimalist Kitchen

WE TRY TO KEEP OUR KITCHEN CLEAN AND SIMPLE IN ORDER TO MAKE COOK-ING and cleanup as fast, efficient, and stress-free as possible. It's taken us many re-evaluations to find a setup that works for us, but we're always looking for ways to streamline and improve.

Our top tips in keeping a minimalist kitchen are to buy quality whenever possible, look for items that perform multiple functions, and keep only what you truly need and use on a daily basis. The rest will inevitably cause clutter and prevent you from getting into the kitchen at all, which is hardly what you want.

For a look at what kitchen appliances and products we use and recommend, check out minimalistbaker.com/simple-kitchen-essentials.

STAPLE PANTRY ITEMS

Keeping a minimalist pantry can sometimes be more difficult than keeping a minimalist kitchen, especially for those of us who love to try new and exciting foods. My top tips are to keep a good organizational system (such as glass jars with labels) and to frequently dispose of products that have expired.

On the next page, you'll find a list of my go-to pantry staples—the ingredients you'll want to keep on hand for preparing the recipes in this cookbook. I've also noted some of my favorite brands. I didn't include produce because it's seasonal and ever-changing.

As with most vegan and gluten-free cooking, feel free to make substitutions as you see fit, according to your dietary needs. Just know that multiple changes to any recipe will almost always vary the outcome of the dish. I recommend avoiding more than one or two ingredient substitutions, and only if you're confident that a substitute ingredient will work well, in order to avoid less-than-desirable outcomes.

NUTS/SEEDS (TRADER JOE'S)	DRY GOODS/PASTA	WET/CANNED GOODS
CHIA + HEMP SEEDS	BROWN RICE	ALMOND MILK (TRADER JOE'S)
FLAXSEED MEAL (BOB'S RED MILL)	GLUTEN-FREE PASTA	BLACK BEANS
RAW ALMONDS, CASHEWS, PECANS + WALNUTS	GLUTEN-FREE ROLLED OATS (TRADER JOE'S)	CHICKPEAS
	LENTILS	CHILI GARLIC SAUCE
ROASTED UNSALTED SUNFLOWER SEEDS	NUTRITIONAL YEAST (WHOLE FOODS BULK SECTION)	COCONUT CREAM (TRADER JOE'S)
SLIVERED ALMONDS		CORN
	QUINOA	DICED TOMATOES
BAKING ESSENTIALS	RICE NOODLES	EXTRA-FIRM SILKEN TOFU (WHOLE FOODS)
APPLE CIDER VINEGAR	SOBA NOODLES	
BAKING POWDER	WHITE RICE	EXTRA-FIRM TOFU (WHOLE FOODS)
BAKING SODA	WHOLE-GRAIN PASTA	
UNSWEETENED APPLESAUCE	**SEASONINGS/SPICES**	FULL-FAT COCONUT MILK (TRADER JOE'S)
VEGAN DARK CHOCOLATE CHIPS (TRADER JOE'S OR ENJOY LIFE FOODS)	BLACK PEPPER	LIGHT COCONUT MILK (TRADER JOE'S)
	CARDAMOM	
	CAYENNE PEPPER	PINTO / REFRIED BEANS
	CHILI POWDER	SOY SAUCE OR TAMARI
SWEETENERS	CINNAMON	TAMARIND CONCENTRATE
AGAVE NECTAR	CORIANDER	TOMATO SAUCE + PASTE
COCONUT SUGAR	CUMIN	VEGAN CREAM CHEESE (TOFUTTI OR TRADER JOE'S)
MAPLE SYRUP	DRIED BASIL	
MEDJOOL DATES	DRIED OREGANO	
ORGANIC BROWN SUGAR	GARAM MASALA	
ORGANIC CANE SUGAR	GARLIC POWDER	**FLOURS/MEALS**
ORGANIC POWDERED/ ICING SUGAR	GREEN CURRY PASTE (THAI KITCHEN)	ALL-PURPOSE FLOUR
		ALMOND MEAL
VEGAN DARK CHOCOLATE	GROUND GINGER	ARROWROOT STARCH
FATS	NUTMEG	BOB'S RED MILL GLUTEN FREE 1-TO-1 BAKING FLOUR
	PUMPKIN PIE SPICE	
AVOCADO OIL	RED CURRY PASTE (THAI AND TRUE)	BROWN + WHITE RICE FLOURS
COCONUT OIL		
GRAPE SEED OIL	SEA SALT	BUCKWHEAT FLOUR
OLIVE OIL	SMOKED PAPRIKA	CORNSTARCH
SESAME OIL	TURMERIC	FINE YELLOW CORNMEAL
VEGAN BUTTER (EARTH BALANCE)		POTATO STARCH
		SEMOLINA FLOUR
		TAPIOCA FLOUR
		WHOLE WHEAT FLOUR
		WHOLE WHEAT PASTRY FLOUR

Nutrition Information

BREAKFAST

Super Green Juice (Page 21)

SERVING SIZE: ¼ OF RECIPE
calories: 84 • total fat: 0g •
saturated fat: 0g • carbohydrates:
20g • sodium: 25mg • fiber: 0.5g •
sugars: 10.3g

Homemade Hippie Cereal (Page 22)

SERVING SIZE: ½ CUP
calories: 175 • total fat: 13.8g •
saturated fat: 1.2g • carbohydrates:
11.2g • sodium: 24mg • fiber: 2.7g •
sugars: 4.6g • protein: 4.3g

Ginger Colada Green Smoothie (Page 25)

SERVING SIZE: 1 SMOOTHIE (OF 2)
calories: 272 • total fat:
14g • saturated fat: 8.9g •
carbohydrates: 35.7g • sodium:
91mg • fiber: 6.2g • sugars: 19.2g •
protein: 5.6g

Beet + Green Apple Yogurt Smoothie (Page 26)

SERVING SIZE: 1 SMOOTHIE (OF 2)
calories: 246 • total fat:
4.6g • saturated fat: 0.5g •
carbohydrates: 44.7g • sodium:
76mg • fiber: 5.2g • sugars: 34g •
protein: 1.5g

Super Powered Chocolate Shake (Page 29)

SERVING SIZE: 1 SHAKE (OF 2)
calories: 176 • total fat: 9.7g •
saturated fat: 1.6g • carbohydrates:
24.4g • sodium: 163mg • fiber: 6.5g
• sugars: 10.4g • protein: 5.3g

Double Chocolate Gluten-Free Waffles (Page 30)

SERVING SIZE: 1 WAFFLE
calories: 419 • total fat:
17.3g • saturated fat: 12.3g •
carbohydrates: 64.7g • sodium:
547mg • fiber: 9.2g • sugars: 15.1g
• protein: 6.4g

Mango Coconut Lassi (Page 33)

SERVING SIZE: 1 SMOOTHIE (OF 2)
calories: 249 • total fat:
7.7g • saturated fat: 6.2g •
carbohydrates: 47.6g • sodium:
90mg • fiber: 7.2g • sugars: 38.3g •
protein: 2g

Spiced Buckwheat Pancakes (Page 34)

SERVING SIZE: 1 PANCAKE
calories: 100 • total fat: 3g •
carbohydrates: 16.8g • sodium:
137mg • fiber: 2.4g • sugars: 3.1g •
protein: 2.7g

Rustic Garlic + Asparagus Tofu Quiche (Page 37)

SERVING SIZE: ⅙ OF RECIPE
calories: 211 • total fat: 7.3g •
saturated fat: 1.2g • carbohydrates:
30.2g • sodium: 366mg • fiber:
5.4g • sugars: 1.6g • protein: 9.4g

Almond Butter + Jelly Granola Bars (Page 40)

SERVING SIZE: 1 GRANOLA BAR
calories: 216 • total fat:
8.5g • saturated fat: 0.7g •
carbohydrates: 33.2g • sodium:
14mg • fiber: 4.7g • sugars: 19.7g •
protein: 5.5g

The Vegan Breakfast Burrito (Page 43)

SERVING SIZE: 1 BURRITO (OF 2)
calories: 869 • total fat:
21.4g • saturated fat: 4.4g •
carbohydrates: 154.3g • sodium:
845mg • fiber: 21g • sugars: 8.8g •
protein: 21g

Savory Eggless Benedict (Page 45)

SERVING SIZE: 1 EGGLESS
BENEDICT WITHOUT SAUCE
calories: 400 • total fat:
27.6g • saturated fat: 5.5g •
carbohydrates: 35g • sodium:
250mg • fiber: 9.1g • sugars: 3.3g •
protein: 7.2g

Serving Size: 2 Tbsp Hollandaise Sauce

calories: 75 • total fat:
5.3g • saturated fat: 0.6g •
carbohydrates: 5.8g • sodium:
78mg • fiber: 1.1g • sugars: 1.6g •
protein: 2g

Pumpkin Chocolate Chip Oat Bread (Page 48)

SERVING SIZE: 1 SLICE (OF 10)
calories: 306 • total fat: 13g •
saturated fat: 7.3g • carbohydrates:
46g • sodium: 352mg • fiber: 5.2g •
sugars: 19.2g • protein: 4.5g

1-Bowl Zucchini Walnut Muffins (Page 51)

SERVING SIZE: 1 MUFFIN
calories: 189 • total fat:
8.4g • saturated fat: 0.9g •
carbohydrates: 27.3g • sodium:
95mg • fiber: 3.1g • sugars: 12.3g •
protein: 3.5g

Banana Chocolate Pecan Muffins (Page 53)

SERVING SIZE: 1 MUFFIN
calories: 269 • total fat: 11.6g •
saturated fat: 5.7g • carbohydrates:
40.2g • sodium: 94mg • fiber: 4.3g
• sugars: 19.1g • protein: 4.6g

Carrot Walnut Bread (Page 56)

SERVING SIZE: 1 SLICE (OF 10)
calories: 260 • total fat: 11.3g •
saturated fat: 1.3g • carbohydrates:
37.5g • sodium: 357mg • fiber: 4.5g
• sugars: 15.7g • protein: 4.4g

Extra Boozy Berry Mimosas (Page 59)

SERVING SIZE: 1 MIMOSA
calories: 198 • total fat: 0.4g •
saturated fat: 0g • carbohydrates:
20.2g • sodium: 5mg • fiber: 1.9g •
sugars: 15.4g

APPETIZERS + SIDES

Orange Moroccan Spiced Nuts (Page 62)

SERVING SIZE: ¼ CUP

calories: 248 • total fat: 22.4g • saturated fat: 4.6g • carbohydrates: 12.3g • sodium: 236mg • fiber: 2.6g • sugars: 8.1g • protein: 3.1g

Pizza-Stuffed Mushrooms (Page 64)

SERVING SIZE: ⅙ OF RECIPE WITH SAUCE

calories: 183 • total fat: 14.1g • saturated fat: 6.1g • carbohydrates: 8.7g • sodium: 494mg • fiber: 2.4g • sugars: 3.4g • protein: 5.5g

Endive Hummus Boats (Page 67)

SERVING SIZE: ⅙ OF RECIPE (2 BITES)*

calories: 128 • total fat: 8.8g • saturated fat: 1g • carbohydrates: 9g • sodium: 300mg • fiber: 4.1g • sugars: 5g • protein: 4g

*Calculated using Roasted Red Pepper + Harissa Hummus

Simple Greek Bruschetta (Page 68)

SERVING SIZE: ⅙ RECIPE (~3 PIECES)

calories: 182 • total fat: 5.5g • saturated fat: 0.8g • carbohydrates: 29.8g • sodium: 403mg • fiber: 1.7g • sugars: 3.8g • protein: 4.7g

Spinach + Artichoke Dip (Page 71)

SERVING SIZE: ⅙ OF RECIPE (~¾ CUP OR 217G)

calories: 336 • total fat: 27.7g • saturated fat: 8.5g • carbohydrates: 17.5g • sodium: 366mg • fiber: 5.7g • sugars: 1.8g • protein: 9.4g

Best Ever 20-Minute Vegan Queso (Page 73)

SERVING SIZE: ⅙ OF RECIPE (~⅓ CUP OR 100G)

calories: 108 • total fat: 6.8g • saturated fat: 2.1g • carbohydrates: 9.7g • sodium: 173mg • fiber: 1.5g • sugars: 2.2g • protein: 2.6g

Roasted Red Pepper + Harissa Hummus (Page 77)

SERVING SIZE: ¼ CUP (47G)

calories: 94 • total fat: 6.9g • saturated fat: 0.9g • carbohydrates: 6.5g • sodium: 155mg • fiber: 0.7g • sugars: 1.8g • protein: 2.2g

Southwest Sweet Potato Black Bean Dip (Page 79)

SERVING SIZE: ⅙ OF RECIPE (200G)

calories: 288 • total fat: 14.3g • saturated fat: 2.4g • carbohydrates: 38.2g • sodium: 98mg • fiber: 7.6g • sugars: 9.7g • protein: 5.2g

Creamy Tomato + Herb Bisque (Page 80)

SERVING SIZE: ¼ OF SOUP RECIPE

Calories: 221 • total fat: 5.5g • saturated fat: 5g • carbohydrates: 39.9g • sodium: 745mg • fiber: 8.4g • sugars: 25.7g • protein: 8.4g

Serving Size: ¼ of Croutons Recipe

calories: 138 • total fat: 11g • saturated fat: 1.1g • carbohydrates: 7.7g • sodium: 236mg • fiber: 1.3g • protein: 2.4g

Simple Sun-Dried Tomato Hummus (Page 82)

SERVING SIZE: ¼ CUP*

calories: 127 • total fat: 9.4g • saturated fat: 1.3g • carbohydrates: 9.8g • sodium: 219mg • fiber: 1.3g • sugars: 1.8g • protein: 3.1g

*Does not include garnish

"Cheddar" Beer Soup (Page 85)

SERVING SIZE: ¼ OF RECIPE*

calories: 299 • total fat: 12.6g • saturated fat: 1.8g • carbohydrates: 36.2g • sodium: 446mg • fiber: 3.6g • sugars: 5g • protein: 8.7g

*Does not include garnish

Creamy Broccoli + "Cheddar" Soup (Page 87)

SERVING SIZE: ¼ OF RECIPE

calories: 206 • total fat: 9.8g • saturated fat: 6.2g • carbohydrates: 24.1g • sodium: 500mg • fiber: 5.9g • sugars: 6.9g • protein: 9.3g

The House Salad (Page 91)

SERVING SIZE: 1 SALAD WITH DRESSING

calories: 221 • total fat: 11.3g • saturated fat: 2g • carbohydrates: 27.9g • sodium: 142mg • fiber: 7.1g • sugars: 13.7g • protein: 5.4g

Balsamic Tomato + Tofu Salad (Page 92)

SERVING SIZE: ¼ OF RECIPE

calories: 69 • total fat: 5g • saturated fat: 0.8g • carbohydrates: 3.5g • sodium: 8mg • fiber: 1.3g • sugars: 1.9g • protein: 3.5g

Coconut Red Curry Vegetable Soup (Page 94)

SERVING SIZE: ¼ OF RECIPE

calories: 237 • total fat: 15.9g • saturated fat: 13.4g • carbohydrates: 24.6g • sodium: 461mg • fiber: 2.1g • sugars: 8g • protein: 4.4g

Greek Kale Salad (Page 96)

SERVING SIZE: ¼ OF RECIPE W/ DRESSING

calories: 169 • total fat: 9.8g • saturated fat: 1.4g • carbohydrates: 17.3g • sodium: 210mg • fiber: 3.2g • sugars: 3.3g • protein: 4.9g

Beet, Orange + Walnut Salad With Lemon Tahini Dressing (Page 99)

SERVING SIZE: ½ OF RECIPE W/ DRESSING

calories: 583 • total fat: 40.2g • saturated fat: 4g • carbohydrates: 49.8g • sodium: 1020mg • fiber: 11.6g • sugars: 33.7g • protein: 15.9g

Garlic "Cheddar" Herb Biscuits (Page 101)

SERVING SIZE: 1 BISCUIT (OF 8)

calories: 181 • total fat: 6.4g • saturated fat: 2.1g • carbohydrates: 25.9g • sodium: 167mg • fiber: 2.1g • protein: 5.2g

Garlic Scalloped Potatoes (Page 103)

SERVING SIZE: ¼ OF RECIPE

calories: 230 • total fat: 9.8g • saturated fat: 1.4g • carbohydrates: 31.6g • sodium: 403mg • fiber: 4.5g • sugars: 1.1g • protein: 7.9g

Raspberry Spinach Ribbon Salad (Page 106)

SERVING SIZE: ¼ OF RECIPE

calories: 446 • total fat: 35.9g • saturated fat: 4.1g • carbohydrates: 25.5g • sodium: 126mg • fiber: 11.5g • sugars: 10.6g • protein: 9.3g

Parmesan Garlic Green Beans (Page 109)

SERVING SIZE: ¼ OF RECIPE

calories: 102 • total fat: 5.6g • saturated fat: 2g • carbohydrates: 9.2g • sodium: 140mg • fiber: 3.9g • sugars: 1.6g • protein: 4.3g

Vegan Kale Caesar Salad (Page 110)

SERVING: ¼ OF RECIPE + 2 TBSP DRESSING

calories: 212 • total fat: 16.3g • saturated fat: 1.4g • carbohydrates: 13.6g • sodium: 290mg • fiber: 1.8g • sugars: 0.6g • protein: 6g

Balsamic + Pomegranate Roasted Sweet Potato Spears (Page 112)

SERVING SIZE: ¼ OF RECIPE

calories: 385 • total fat: 21.6g • saturated fat: 4.8g • carbohydrates: 44.8g • sodium: 131mg • fiber: 7.8g • sugars: 9.2g • protein: 4.7g

MAIN DISHES

White Bean Posole Verde (Page 117)

SERVING SIZE: ¼ OF RECIPE*

calories: 227 • total fat: 9.2g • saturated fat: 1.1g • carbohydrates: 44g • sodium: 400mg • fiber: 9.9g • sugars: 5.3g • protein: 10.3g

*Does not include topping options.

Super-Thick Three-Bean Chili (Page 120)

SERVING SIZE: ⅙ OF RECIPE*

calories: 337 • total fat: 4.6g • saturated fat: 0.5g • carbohydrates: 65.5g • sodium: 816mg • fiber: 11.9g • sugars: 14.5g • protein: 11.9g

*Does not include serving options.

Cornbread Chili Pot Pies (Page 122)

SERVING SIZE: ⅙ OF RECIPE

calories: 480 • total fat: 14.7g • saturated fat: 3.8g • carbohydrates: 77.1g • sodium: 1724mg • fiber: 10.6g • sugars: 19.2g • protein: 12g

Chickpea Fesenjan (Page 124)

SERVING SIZE: ¼ OF RECIPE*

calories: 515 • total fat: 35.1g • saturated fat: 2.5g • carbohydrates: 41.2g • sodium: 279mg • fiber: 7.5g • sugars: 18.9g • protein: 15.7g

*Does not include toppings or rice.

Simple Curried Carrot + Lentil Soup (Page 126)

SERVING SIZE: ¼ OF RECIPE

calories: 369 • total fat: 12.8g • saturated fat: 8.8g • carbohydrates: 51.5g • sodium:

497mg • fiber: 16.7g • sugars: 13.1g • protein: 14.5g

Masala Chickpea Curry (Page 129)

SERVING SIZE: ¼ OF RECIPE*

calories: 379 • total fat: 24.5g • saturated fat: 20.2g • carbohydrates: 39g • sodium: 340mg • fiber: 6.3g • sugars: 15.8g • protein: 8.1g

*Does not include serving options.

Carrot, Potato + Chickpea Red Curry (Page 131)

SERVING SIZE: ¼ OF RECIPE*

calories: 345 • total fat: 12.3g • saturated fat: 2.5g • carbohydrates: 52.7g • sodium: 1016mg • fiber: 6.3g • sugars: 18.7g • protein: 7.8g

*Does not include optional toppings.

1-Pot Chickpea Noodle Soup (Page 135)

SERVING SIZE: ⅙ OF RECIPE

calories: 272 • total fat: 6.6g • saturated fat: 0.7g • carbohydrates: 48.4g • sodium: 251mg • fiber: 5.7g • sugars: 3.9g • protein: 6.3g

Butternut Squash, Kale + Quinoa Bake (Page 136)

SERVING SIZE: ⅙ OF RECIPE

calories: 265 • total fat: 12.9g • saturated fat: 1.1g • carbohydrates: 31.1g • sodium: 76mg • fiber: 5.3g • sugars: 3.2g • protein: 9.5g

Roasted Chickpea Tabbouleh Salad (Page 139)

SERVING SIZE: ¼ OF RECIPE

calories: 293 • total fat: 18.9g • saturated fat: 4.1g • carbohydrates: 26.8g • sodium: 472mg • fiber: 3.7g • sugars: 9.4g • protein: 7.5g

Easy Weeknight Burrito Bowls (Page 141)

SERVING SIZE: ¼ OF RECIPE

calories: 449 • total fat: 14.3g • saturated fat: 2.5g • carbohydrates: 72.5g • sodium: 428mg • fiber: 10.3g • sugars: 5.2g • protein: 10.8g

Garlic Pineapple Stir-Fried Quinoa (Page 145)

SERVING SIZE: ¼ OF RECIPE

calories: 525 • total fat: 26g • saturated fat: 4.1g • carbohydrates: 63g • sodium: 1081mg • fiber: 6.6g • sugars: 18.6g • protein: 15.6g

Cashew Soba Noodle Salad (Page 146)

SERVING: ¼ OF RECIPE W/ DRESSING

calories: 501 • total fat: 23g • saturated fat: 4.4g • carbohydrates: 61.2g • sodium: 1012mg • fiber: 4.8g • sugars: 18.3g • protein: 18.4g

Thai Baked Sweet Potatoes (Page 149)

SERVING SIZE: ¼ OF RECIPE

calories: 435 • total fat: 14g • saturated fat: 3.2g • carbohydrates: 71.3g • sodium: 880mg • fiber: 7.8g • sugars: 14.1g • protein: 9.5g

Spicy Tofu Vegetable Stir-Fry (Page 151)

SERVING SIZE: ½ OF RECIPE

calories: 357 • total fat: 13.3g • saturated fat: 2.2g • carbohydrates: 49.3g • sodium: 2013mg • fiber: 6.2g • sugars: 29.1g • protein: 17.6g

Vegan Cobb Salad (Page 154)

SERVING SIZE: ¼ OF RECIPE*

calories: 316 • total fat: 18g • saturated fat: 2.9g • carbohydrates: 32.9g • sodium: 169mg • fiber: 6.9g • sugars: 4.8g • protein: 9g

*Does not include dressing.

Better-Than-Restaurant Vegan Nachos (Page 156)

SERVING SIZE: ¼ OF RECIPE

calories: 590 • total fat: 24.4g • saturated fat: 5.8g • carbohydrates: 83.6g • sodium: 1187mg • fiber: 16.7g • sugars: 3.2g • protein: 15.3g

Spicy Braised Tofu Tostadas (Page 159)

SERVING SIZE: 1 TOSTADA (OF 6)*

calories: 184 • total fat: 10.1g • saturated fat: 1.4g • carbohydrates: 19.2g • sodium: 195mg • fiber: 2.5g • sugars: 2.9g • protein: 6.4g

*Does not include optional toppings.

The Best Vegan Enchiladas (Page 161)

SERVING SIZE: 2 ENCHILADAS*

calories: 349 • total fat: 6.8g • carbohydrates: 60.6g • sodium: 141mg • fiber: 11.5g • sugars: 12g • protein: 13.1g

*Does not include optional toppings.

Smashed Black Bean Green Chili Taquitos (Page 164)

SERVING SIZE: 1 TAQUITO (OF 10)

calories: 147 • total fat: 3g • carbohydrates: 27.4g • sodium: 179mg • fiber: 5.4g • sugars: 4.8g • protein: 4.7g

Vegan "No Tuna" Salad Sandwich (Page 167)

SERVING SIZE: 1 SANDWICH WITH BREAD*

calories: 326 • total fat: 5.7g • saturated fat: 1g • carbohydrates: 53.7g • sodium: 473mg • fiber: 4.8g • sugars: 9.2g • protein: 14.8g

The Trashy Vegan Sandwich (Page 168)

SERVING SIZE: 1 SANDWICH

calories: 544 • total fat: 32.3g • saturated fat: 4.4g • carbohydrates: 52.9g • sodium: 1089mg • fiber: 13g • sugars: 10.6g • protein: 14.8g

Thai Quinoa Meatballs (Page 171)

SERVING SIZE: 6 MEATBALLS*

calories: 441 • total fat: 21.2g • saturated fat: 3g • carbohydrates: 49.3g • sodium: 831mg • fiber: 5.8g • sugars: 17.9g • protein: 17.9g

*Does not include serving options.

Hearty Cocoa Black Bean Burgers (Page 173)

SERVING SIZE: ¼ OF RECIPE*

calories: 430 • total fat: 27.2g • saturated fat: 2.6g • carbohydrates: 38.7g • sodium: 323mg • fiber: 9.7g • sugars: 4.8g • protein: 15.8g

*Does not include additional toppings.

Thai Peanut Burgers (Page 176)

SIZE: 1 BURGER (OF 4)*

calories: 506 • total fat: 20.4g • saturated fat: 2.8g • carbohydrates: 63.1g • sodium: 244mg • fiber: 6.5g • sugars: 15g • protein: 20.6g

*Does not include serving options.

Spicy BBQ Jackfruit Sandwiches with Grilled Pineapple (Page 179)

SERVING SIZE: 1 SANDWICH WITH BUN*

calories: 351 • total fat: 9.1g • saturated fat: 1.2g • carbohydrates: 62.5g • sodium: 1176mg • fiber: 6g • sugars: 32.4g • protein: 5.1g

Pizza Burgers (Page 181)

SERVING SIZE: 1 BURGER*

calories: 296 • total fat: 15g • saturated fat: 2.3g • carbohydrates: 33.8g • sodium: 482mg • fiber: 2.4g • sugars: 6.3g • protein: 8.8g

*Does not include serving options.

Smoky BBQ Veggie Burgers (Page 185)

SERVING SIZE: ¼ OF RECIPE*

calories: 388 • total fat: 15.1g • saturated fat: 9.4g • carbohydrates: 53.5g • sodium: 477mg • fiber: 8.6g • sugars: 7.0g • protein: 11.9g

*Does not include serving options.

Deep-Dish Pizza with Tofu Ricotta (Page 187)

SERVING SIZE: ¼ OF RECIPE*

calories: 421 • total fat: 11.9g • saturated fat: 1.8g • carbohydrates: 63.7g • sodium: 678mg • fiber: 4.6g • sugars: 4.7g • protein: 15.1g

*Estimate made using ⅔ of the tofu ricotta filling.

Angel Hair Pasta With Harissa Romesco (Page 190)

calories: 471 • total fat: 26.7g • saturated fat: 3.1g • carbohydrates: 49.2g • sodium: 272mg • fiber: 2.3g • sugars: 5.6g • protein: 11.8g

Does not include optional toppings.

Butternut Squash Garlic Mac 'N' Cheese (Page 193)

SERVING SIZE: ¼ OF RECIPE* calories: 313 • total fat: 8.8g • saturated fat: 0.7g • carbohydrates: 55.6g • sodium: 194mg • fiber: 6g • sugars: 1.5g • protein: 5.9g

Does not include serving options.

Peanut Butter Pad Thai (Page 195)

SERVING SIZE: ¼ OF RECIPE* calories: 231 • total fat: 7.6g • saturated fat: 1.1g • carbohydrates: 32.4g • sodium: 775mg • fiber: 4.2g • sugars: 12.8g • protein: 11.2g

Does not include serving options.

Sweet Potato Sage Raviolis (Page 199)

SERVING SIZE: ⅙ OF RECIPE calories: 444 • total fat: 13.6g • saturated fat: 1.5g • carbohydrates: 69.3g • sodium: 85mg • fiber: 5.7g • sugars: 4.5g • protein: 12.6g

Herb-Marinated Tofu (Page 203)

SERVING SIZE: 1/7 OF RECIPE calories: 177 • total fat: 16.9g • saturated fat: 2.6g • carbohydrates: 3.7g • sodium: 677mg • fiber: 0.8g • sugars: 2.3g • protein: 6g

Simple Tomato + Lentil Ragu (Page 205)

SERVING SIZE: ¼ OF RECIPE* calories: 196 • total fat: 4.3g • saturated fat: 0.6g • carbohydrates: 33g • sodium: 1055mg • fiber: 11.6g • sugars: 13.4g • protein: 9.6g

Does not include serving options.

Classic Vegan Lasagna (Page 207)

SERVING SIZE: 1 SQUARE (OF 9) calories: 326 • total fat: 10.4g • saturated fat: 1.8g • carbohydrates: 46.5g • sodium: 448mg • fiber: 3g • sugars: 7.7g • protein: 12.7g

DESSERTS

Toasted Coconut Dark Chocolate Popcorn (Page 213)

SERVING SIZE: ⅛ OF RECIPE calories: 430 • total fat: 19.4g • saturated fat: 13.1g • carbohydrates: 64.9g • sodium: 14mg • fiber: 15.1g • sugars: 14g • protein: 9.1g

5-Ingredient Peppermint Patties (Page 214)

SERVING SIZE: 1 PATTY (OF 14) calories: 122 • total fat: 9.4g • saturated fat: 7.5g • carbohydrates: 9.1g • sodium: 4mg • fiber: 1.5g • sugars: 6.1g • protein: 1.2g

1-Bowl Jumbo Chocolate Chip Cookies (Page 216)

SERVING SIZE: 1 COOKIE (OF 12) calories: 216 • total fat: 9.4g • saturated fat: 3.6g • carbohydrates: 30.3g • sodium: 374mg • fiber: 1.1g • sugars: 16g • protein: 2.3g

Dark Chocolate Almond Coconut Bites (Page 219)

SERVING SIZE: 1 BITE (OF 20) calories: 126 • total fat: 9.9g • saturated fat: 8g • carbohydrates: 7.2g • sodium: 9mg • fiber: 2.3g • sugars: 4.6g • protein: 1.6g

Chocolate-Dunked Peanut Butter Cookies (Page 223)

SERVING SIZE: 1 COOKIE (OF 20) calories: 183 • total fat: 9.9g • saturated fat: 3.3g • carbohydrates: 20.5g • sodium: 246mg • fiber: 1.2g • sugars: 12.5g • protein: 3.2g

Blackberry Custard Pie (Page 225)

SERVING SIZE: 1 SLICE (OF 8) calories: 320 • total fat: 17.9g • saturated fat: 7.6g • carbohydrates: 35.6g • sodium: 279mg • fiber: 3.2g • sugars: 13.7g • protein: 4.9g

Blender Sweet Potato Pie (Page 229)

SERVING SIZE: 1 SLICE (OF 8)* calories: 337 • total fat: 12g • saturated fat: 3.8g • carbohydrates: 52.8g • sodium: 293mg • fiber: 2.2g • sugars: 16.9g • protein: 4.2g

Does not include toppings

1-Bowl Vegan Tiramisu Cake (Page 231)

SERVING SIZE: 1 SLICE (OF 9) calories: 437 • total fat: 25.9g • saturated fat: 15.2g • carbohydrates: 47.3g • sodium: 1176mg • fiber: 1.7g • sugars: 27.3g • protein: 4.1g

Apricot Hand Pies (Page 235)

SERVING SIZE: 1 PIE (OF 10) calories: 222 • total fat: 12.1g • saturated fat: 4.3g • carbohydrates: 24.9g • sodium: 196mg • fiber: 1g • sugars: 4.8g • protein: 2.8g

Pumpkin Apple Upside-Down Cake (Page 239)

SERVING SIZE: 1 SLICE (OF 10) calories: 211 • total fat: 8.1g • saturated fat: 2.2g • carbohydrates: 33.7g • sodium: 506mg • fiber: 2.1g • sugars: 18.2g • protein: 2.3g

Vegan Vanilla Cupcakes (Page 241)

SERVING SIZE: 1 CUPCAKE (OF 12) calories: 354 • total fat: 20.4g • saturated fat: 11g • carbohydrates: 42g • sodium: 696mg • fiber: 2.9g • sugars: 26.9g • protein: 3g

Strawberry Swirl Ice Cream (Page 244)

SERVING SIZE: ½ CUP (OF 8)
calories: 332 • total fat:
24.8g • saturated fat: 9.4g •
carbohydrates: 27.3g • sodium:
163mg • fiber: 1.7g • sugars: 18.2g •
protein: 4.3g

Peanut Butter + Jelly Ice Cream Sandwiches (Page 247)

SERVING SIZE: 1 SANDWICH
calories: 361 • total fat:
26g • saturated fat: 5.9g •
carbohydrates: 25.1g • sodium:
111mg • fiber: 5g • sugars: 15.3g •
protein: 10.6g

Cherry Chia Lassi Pops (Page 248)

SERVING SIZE: 1 POPSICLE (OF 10)
calories: 77 • total fat:
3.8g • saturated fat: 2.6g •
carbohydrates: 9.5g • sodium:
5mg • fiber: 0.7g • sugars: 7.9g •
protein: 1.9g

Peanut Butter Fudge Swirl Ice Cream (Page 251)

SERVING SIZE: ½ CUP (OF 7)
calories: 482 • total fat: 35.8g •
saturated fat: 16g • carbohydrates:
34.6g • sodium: 420mg • fiber: 3.1g
• sugars: 24.5g • protein: 8.3g

Double Chocolate Skillet Bread Pudding (Page 253)

SERVING SIZE: ⅙ OF RECIPE
calories: 363 • total fat:
13.1g • saturated fat: 8.3g •
carbohydrates: 52.1g • sodium:
336mg • fiber: 6.1g • sugars: 27.7g •
protein: 12.4g

Peanut Butter Cup Puffed Rice Bars (Page 256)

SERVING SIZE: 1 BAR (OF 16)
calories: 190 • total fat:
10.8g • saturated fat: 2.9g •
carbohydrates: 20.4g • sodium:
47mg • fiber: 1.7g • sugars: 13.1g •
protein: 5.1g

No-Bake Strawberry Cheesecake Bars (Page 259)

SERVING SIZE: 1 BAR (OF 12)*
calories: 205 • total fat:
14.6g • saturated fat: 5.6g •
carbohydrates: 17.6g • sodium:
10mg • fiber: 0.9g • sugars: 11.4g •
protein: 2.8g

*Includes strawberry topping and
calculated using full-fat coconut milk.

Cherry Chocolate Chip Ice Cream (Page 261)

SERVING SIZE: ½ CUP (OF 10)
calories: 306 • total fat:
21.8g • saturated fat: 10.4g •
carbohydrates: 26g • sodium:
38mg • fiber: 0.7g • sugars: 17.9g •
protein: 3.9g

Coconut Sugar Caramel Sauce (Page 265)

SERVING SIZE: 2 TABLESPOONS
calories: 69 • total fat: 2.4g •
saturated fat: 2.1g • carbohydrates:
12.6g • sodium: 33mg • sugars:
12.4g • protein: 0.2g

BEVERAGES

Pumpkin Chai Tea Lattes (Page 269)

SERVING SIZE: 1 GLASS (OF 2)
calories: 130 • total fat: 3.6g •
carbohydrates: 25g • sodium:
184mg • fiber: 2.3g • sugars: 19.3g
• protein: 1.8g

Fresh-Pressed Apple Cider (Page 270)

SERVING SIZE: 1 GLASS (OF 9)
calories: 86 • total fat: 0.3g •
carbohydrates: 22.8g • sodium:
3mg • fiber: 3.8g • sugars: 17.2g •
protein: 0.5g

Creamy Vegan Eggnog (Page 272)

SERVING SIZE: 1 GLASS (OF 9)
calories: 204 • total fat:
14.4g • saturated fat: 4.9g •
carbohydrates: 17.4g • sodium:
44mg • fiber: 1.2g • sugars: 9.5g •
protein: 4.1g

Simple Tamarind Whiskey Sour (Page 274)

SERVING SIZE: 1 GLASS
calories: 85 • total fat: 0.1g •
carbohydrates: 21.7g • sodium:
878mg • sugars: 17.6g • protein:
0.6g

Sparkling Peach + Berry White Sangria (Page 277)

SERVING SIZE: 1 GLASS
calories: 235 • total fat: 0.3g •
carbohydrates: 13.3g • sodium:
213mg • fiber: 2g • sugars: 27.5g •
protein: 0.8g

Recipe Index

ACKNOWLEDGMENTS

We couldn't have made this cookbook without the support of our readers who allow us to do the work we love. To our fans: we love you to the moon and back.

To the readers who graciously volunteered to test and give feedback for each and every recipe: thank you, thank you, thank you! You made the dishes in this book the best they could possibly be.

To our designer, Holly Whittlef: you make us look so good and put together, and we're oh so thankful for you.

To our relentless editor and close friend, Jamin Still: thank you for refining and perfecting the pages of this book amid a season of new fatherhood. We love you.

To John: thank you for letting us sell our couch to buy our first digital camera, for telling me, "You can totally do this," and for just generally believing in me. Thank you—I love you.

And last, thank you to friends and family who have supported us along this crazy journey, despite never really knowing if (or how) we were going to make this haphazard career on the Internet work. We love you.

ABOUT US

Dana Shultz is the recipe developer and author
of the simple food blog Minimalist Baker, which she
founded with her husband, John, in 2012.

Together the pair is a blogging match made in heaven.
Dana creates the recipes, the photographs, and the
blog content, while John designs, codes, develops
products, and plays visionary.

The couple is situated in Portland, Oregon, where they
indulge in all the craft coffee, wine, and food they
can get their hands on. Though they call the Pacific
Northwest home, they suffer from an insatiable need
for adventure, and enjoy traveling often. Naturally,
it's usually for great food.